FRONTSTALAG 142

❖

*The Internment Diary
of an English Lady*

Mabel Fanny Twemlow
1881-1990

Aunt Fan on the garden steps in Ciboure, Pyrénées-Atlantiques, in about 1950.

FRONTSTALAG 142

❧

The Internment Diary
of an English Lady

KATHERINE LACK

AMBERLEY

First published 2010

Amberley Publishing Plc
Cirencester Road, Chalford,
Stroud, Gloucestershire, GL6 8PE

www.amberley-books.com

Copyright © Katherine Lack, 2010

The right of Katherine Lack to be identified as the Author
of this work has been asserted in accordance with the
Copyrights, Designs and Patents Act 1988.

British Library Cataloguing in Publication Data.
A catalogue record for this book is available from the British Library.

ISBN 978-1-4456-0055-0

Typesetting and Origination by Amberley Publishing.
Printed in Great Britain.

Contents

Dedicated to the memory of all those who were
interned in the camps at Besançon and Vittel,
with grateful thanks to everyone who helped them.

A proportion of the proceeds from this book
will be donated to the work of
The International Red Cross.

Acknowledgements

A book of this kind will always be a collaborative work, and it gives me great pleasure to thank those who have contributed. Any errors, however, remain mine alone.

First, and most important, my mother-in-law Mrs Elizabeth Lack, Aunt Fan's niece, has treasured the diary and collection of pictures from the camps for many years, and gladly gave permission for them to be published.

During the field work visits to Besançon and Vittel, I was greatly assisted by Mrs Sally Jones, not least because of her fluency in French. The administrative staff of l'Hôpital St Jacques at Besançon, the archivists at Le Centre de Documentation of the Musée de la Résistance et de la Déportation at the Citadel in Besançon, and Mme Jacqueline Verrier of the Maison du Patrimoine at Vittel, all gave invaluable help.

Permission to use the pictures from the Vittel camp was given by La Maison du Patrimoine de Vittel. For permission to use quotations from internment memoirs and papers, I would like to thank the Trustees of the Imperial War Museum in London, the Besançon Centre de Documentation, and the respective individual copyright holders. Extracts from *Red Princess* are courtesy of Ms Sofka Zinovieff and Granta Publications. The quotation from Rosemary Say is courtesy of Julia Holland: the full story of Rosemary's internment and escape is to be published in *Rosie's War*, Michael O'Mara Books, 2011. Every effort has been made to trace copyright holders for the material used; further information would be welcomed and any omissions will be rectified in any future editions.

During the course of the preparation of this book, I have been in touch with many people who have an interest in the internment camps at Besançon and Vittel. Some are the last survivors of the camps, who have contacted me with personal stories of their wartime experiences. Others are relatives of internees. I am most grateful to all of the following for their various contributions: Mme Anna Bourne, Geoffrey Constable, James Fox, Mrs Gould-Smith, Mlle Sonia Gumuchian, John and Christopher Hales, Roger Horton, Sister Dorothy Kerr, Mike Maranian, Mrs Janet Maxwell Stewart, Mme Fernande Oldfield, Dr Steffen Prauser, Miss Ann Rose (who supplied the picture of the mat from Besançon), Dr Mike Snape, M. Jean-Louis and the late Mme Madeleine Steinberg, Doyle Twemlow and Ms Sofka Zinovieff.

Last but by no means least, a special thank you is due to my husband Paul who, as ever, helped with the photography and gave considerable practical and moral support.

I

'Aunt Fan' – An Introduction

I first met Aunt Fan when she was 101, when I married her great-nephew. She was still a tall, imposing lady, and although nearly blind and extremely deaf, she remained a formidable character with a wicked sense of humour. She was somewhat ill-at-ease in England, having recently moved from her beloved home in the south of France to live with my mother-in-law, her niece. She had been persuaded that she should no longer be living alone, especially as she was recovering from breaking her leg. So she had uprooted herself from St Jean-de-Luz where she had lived for over eighty years, and the family home had been sold. However, she was relatively comfortable with members of the armed services, and as I was the daughter of a naval officer, this perhaps explained why we got on so well. Besides, as she often said with a twinkle, 'Every nice girl loves a sailor'.

Aunt Fan had kept a diary during the Second World War, but although I knew this, I only made time to read it after she had died. When I did, I soon discovered that it was not, as I had imagined, merely an account of rationing and minor privation among the affluent expatriate community in France. Instead, it told a remarkable story of her internment by the German army of occupation, the conditions suffered by the prisoners, and her eventual release and return home.

The family was keen for the diary to be preserved, and happy for me to edit it and get it published. But therein lay a problem. The diary itself was suspiciously understated, and from what little I knew of Aunt Fan, I suspected that it only hinted at the real conditions in the camps. Some additional material was available from tape-recordings my husband had encouraged her to make of her reminiscences, and from a series of notebooks she had filled with rather disconnected jottings in her extreme old age. Even these, however, revealed more stiff upper lip than self-pity. Indeed, she specifically told her relations that she did not want the difficulties she had faced to be exaggerated in any way.

For more insights, I had to look for other accounts of the internment camps, and I was fortunate to find several such memoirs; some deposited in archives in Britain and France, and others handed down to the internees' relations and friends. I was also eventually able to get in touch with some of the last survivors themselves, one of whom, to our mutual delight, remembered Aunt Fan herself, despite their great difference in age, because of their shared love of art. This kind and courteous lady was also able to identify some of the individuals who had sat for Aunt Fan's sketches in the camps. The great generosity of all these people in reopening this painful chapter of their lives so that the story could be told cannot be underestimated. One of the most poignant moments in my research was to make contact with a family in England whose aunt had been interned in the same room as Aunt Fan, and who still possess a small piece of cloth with Aunt Fan's name embroidered on it.

As to Aunt Fan herself, I already knew from my forays into family history that she came from a very comfortable middle-class background. In fact, she was the daughter and grand-daughter of generals. Her grandfather George Twemlow served with the Royal Bengal Artillery and married Anna D'Oyley in Calcutta in 1825. Their son Edward D'Oyley Twemlow (1840-1936), Aunt Fan's father, was born in India and became a major-general in the Royal Engineers. Much of his career was spent building bridges and railways for the army in India and Afghanistan, and several of his children were born abroad. I discovered from Aunt Fan's notebooks that his wife, Margaret Anne Blanche Corrie, had progressive ideas and allowed her daughters considerable freedom, although she herself had been raised more conventionally:

> She was the third child in a family of twelve, born in 1847 and was brought up as girls were in that generation. Her father played the cello and several of the sons and girls played violins etc. My mother played the piano very well and also the harp. She played dances, hymns and songs for us.

By her own admission, Aunt Fan never thought much about cooking until their last maid died, and it was her proud boast that she had never washed a sheet in her life. How would a lady from such a background, raised in antique gentility, cope with life in a prison camp? Fortunately, the notebooks and tapes contain many reminiscences about her life both before and during the War, and help to construct a picture of someone who spent many happy hours as a child playing out of doors with her brother, despite the impediments of long skirts and a compulsory hat. They reveal a young lady as comfortable with a horse as on a bicycle – to the horror of the neighbours. Aged about twelve, she asked her mother if she was allowed to go off with her friend's brother to learn to ride a bicycle; later, she enquired why her mother had given her permission so readily, to which her mother replied, 'Oh, I knew you would do it anyhow, so I just said yes!' Throughout, one can hear echoes of a character of steely determination and fearless practicality which is only hinted at in the diary.

Aunt Fan lived to the age of 108, fully lucid until the last two months, which suggests that the Third Reich made a grave miscalculation in releasing her from internment when she reached sixty.

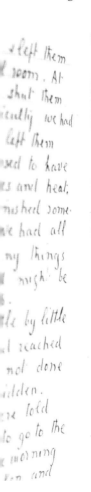

A page of Aunt Fan's internment diary.

2

To France

Aunt Fan's childhood was not all joy. While her parents continued to live in India, she was boarded out for two years in England with her sister Kathleen and their younger brother Hubert; an experience that she remembered vividly and uncomfortably to the end of her life:

I remember being in Aden [aged three] and the war in Egypt was raging and we had a few hours notice that a P & O carrying troops from India would pick us up – my mother and her 3 children and her sister and a nurse – and take us back to England. Then in the Bay of Biscay I fell out of my berth and cut my head over my eye. I very well remember that my mother was lying on the floor, with the baby and the nurse also on the floor. She told me to go round to the doctor. Well, I seemed to be perfectly happy. I went round, it must have been close by. And I found the doctor lying on the floor! He sat up, he didn't stand, and he brought out a little book of plasters in 3 different colours, and he asked me which colour I would like. So I said 'Black,' because it would show up well. And so he plastered up my head with black, and I paraded every day with my black patch – I was very proud of it!

After that I don't remember much until we were left with a doctor's family, and Mother went back to India. I was five then, my brother was 18 months younger and my sister was a little older. We suddenly realised that Mother seemed very unhappy and she was going away, and we all sat down on the floor and burst into tears. Mother was leaving our old nurse with us, a motherly old woman as far as I remember. Well, I suppose we cheered up, but we were there for 2 years, and the first thing that happened was that our old nurse was dismissed, and a nursemaid came. And from that time on I don't remember anything very happy. We were kept in the nursery.

For a quiet child, I often seemed to be getting into trouble. I stole a lump of sugar and hid it under the table, and I was punished for that – I had to say the commandment 'Thou shalt not steal' every Sunday. But it was a big house, and we used to play at the top of the house, where my sister and I slept alone. And I had to go upstairs alone in the dark and of course I was simply terrified of all sorts of bogies.

In the spare room we found a skeleton of a man, wrapped up in a sheet! Well, this amused us, and we managed to pull out his teeth. But when this was found out, of course, there were more punishments. And one night, when I went up to bed, and took my usual flying leap into bed, because there was always SOMETHING under the bed I thought, the skeleton was in the bed, wrapped in a shawl! I don't know who put it there, probably one of the doctor's older boys. Well, I was more afraid of the bogies under the bed than I was of that skeleton, so I threw him out onto the floor and waited for my sister to come up to bed. But I don't think she moved the skeleton, either – I don't know what happened. More punishments for ill-treating the skeleton!

Then another time I knocked over a lamp in the hall, and set fire to the carpet. The governess was with the doctor's two older children and Kathleen in the dining room, which they used as their school room, and I didn't know what to do. The flames were running along the carpet and had got to the staircase. So I seized the dinner gong and rang it. The governess came out, furious, and then saw what was happening. She certainly kept her head very well, because she sent us all running for rugs and we put out the flames. What happened to me after that I don't know.

But of course all this left my brother and me the most frightened kind of children. And so when my mother took us back after 2 years she was amazed to find that we were both so nervous. We wouldn't go into a dark room, or sleep alone, or anything. And I was then over 7 years old [1888].

Mother came to fetch us. I don't remember leaving, or the journey, but there were no tears, I'm sure. But we were very excited, because we knew we had another sister, 2 years old. So when we arrived at the house where Mother was staying, we went in to see this new sister. She was sitting on the floor surrounded by toys, and she wouldn't let us touch any of them. And when we talked to Mother she rushed to us and kicked us! She said 'She's NOT your mother, she's mine!' And so we came to the conclusion that we were very disappointed; she was a horrid little thing and we would have no more to do with her. Of course that wore off, and she gave in and accepted that we had to share our mother.

Having a mother was our greatest joy. She read to us, gave us lessons in astronomy, natural history, music. Our only fear now was that she might die and that we would be alone again.

The next child, born in England in 1892, was a handicapped girl who was christened Victoria Margaret but always known in the family as Molly:

> Molly made slow progress as a baby. Any noise made her cry, and we learnt to be quiet in the house. Mother took her to see a specialist in London – he thought she would never learn to walk. Baby grew up quite perfect in body, though not in mind. She looked like a child of 10 all her life and lived for 60 years.

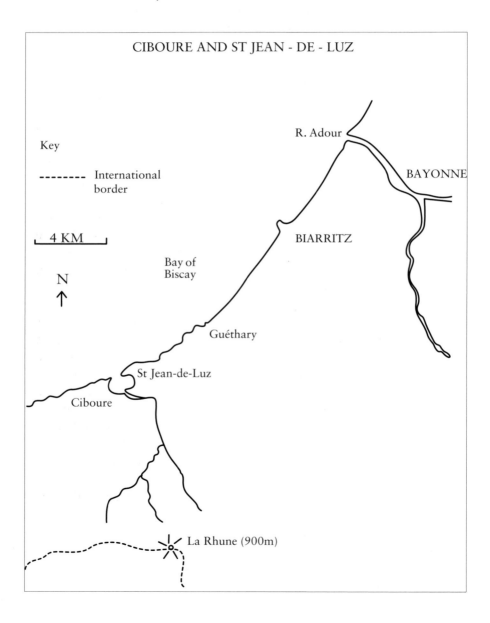

There were other family sadnesses too. Alfred, the youngest child, fell ill suddenly after a day playing happily on the beach, and died within the week, aged seven. Fan's oldest brother was invalided home from the Boer War, and in 1905 her favourite brother Hubert, who by then was a lieutenant in the 89th Punjabis, was fatally shot in an accident on a firing range at Mandalay. But back in 1893, when their father retired early from the army, the family was briefly reunited:

Father came home on sick leave and did not return to India again. I believe he was due to retire. Our new house in Winchester had a good garden and a tennis court. After some weeks in bed taking only milk Father recovered – he took up golf and read philosophy. He was a Liberal. Each winter he had a recurrence of the illness "sprue" [a tropical variant of the 'thrush' infection of the mouth, causing chronic digestive problems] and doctors said he should go to a milder climate. So it was decided to sell the house and the whole family go to S. W. France to St Jean de Luz – recommended by a fellow Royal Engineer who had settled there.

Mother and I went in advance via Paris, and Father and Kathleen with the three younger children, 3 bicycles and a ton of luggage, came by sea to Bordeaux and then by train. Mother and I went to a pension [boarding house] for a few days. An agent in St Jean had taken a villa for us outside the town on a hill, the biggest he could get, and we engaged two Basque maids. It was fully furnished, and I think the rent was £100 for the year. We arrived Oct 4th 1900, and we never had a residence in England again. Father never had a recurrence of the disease, and he lived to be 95.

There were a good many English residents and visitors in St Jean at that time. We soon had many friends both English and American. The French were not so friendly – the Boer War, the difference in religion, but also French girls were brought up so strictly that they were not allowed to meet us. Their brothers could play tennis or go to picnic with us.

We enjoyed ourselves very much. We climbed La Rhune (3000 feet) the nearest Pyrenean mountain, bathed in the sea and explored the country on bicycles. We went into Spain – no passports necessary – and bought oranges at 2 sous each. The roads were dusty and our bicycles had no lights, but the only traffic was oxcarts, women on donkeys, sometimes a big wagon and a string of mules.

My sister Kathleen and I now began to think of doing something to make a little money. We easily found pupils for English and painting. Two girls I taught aged 19 & 21 never went out alone & went twice to church every day. Kathleen taught several English children. Dora [their younger sister, Theodora] went to a small English school. We all took lessons in Spanish.

Molly by this time was about 12 years old. She picked up French very quickly, but could neither read nor write. She was very fond of music, and sang songs and hymns. I tried to teach her the piano, but gave it up: she had small hands and feet, although all in proportion to her height. We took her for walks and our two maids were very fond of her and helped us in every way. Then we met an English lady who ran a small school and she said she would try to teach Molly. So we left her there for three winters and she learned to read and also to play hymns and songs for the other pupils, and to sing to her own accompaniment. She liked to make up tunes. But then she was getting homesick, so we decided to keep her at home. She could now amuse herself with simple books. She also liked to read Paradise Lost and Shakespeare, but without understanding a word, I think – she liked long words.

I was painting more seriously and began selling sketches for one or two pounds, also Christmas cards. My sister and I realised that if we did not marry, we would have only £60 a year pension. We did not worry, as a pound went a long way in those days.

In 1910 I had a picture in the Paris Salon, a picture of the convent where Chopin lived, and for about 10 years I also sent to the Geneva Salon and only stopped when my very nice Agent died. I illustrated a book on Basque architecture for an American, and did bookbinding for the Biarritz Antiquarian Society and private customers.

Since 1910 I had rented a cottage in Ciboure, the fishing village the other side of the harbour. I generally made the rent by pictures of the kitchen with its open hearth and tiny windows. I often stayed there at night and sometimes took my sister Molly there for a change. From this cottage I could see ... a neglected garden on a steep slope towards the south east, with a lovely view of mountain and valley. A perfect place for a house, and finding it was for sale I suggested to my Father that we should buy it and build a house ... Father saw to all the specification – it was an excellent house, with a terrace and a balcony, a flight of steps down to the garden & a lovely view. We moved in in 1926 – my Father was then 86. In fact my parents never left it – both died before the 2nd War – both over 90.

In 1912, Dora was married and in 1914 the church bells rang out to tell us France had declared war on Germany. The old Hospice, which had been built for pilgrims to Compostella, was used for refugees. Hundreds arrived, men, children and women.

Very soon the Hospice was cleared and cleaned up a bit, anyhow one big ward and several smaller – still no electric light or water and one tap in the kitchen down below, which had lots of black beetles and rats. Soldiers now came, mostly Belgians. They slept in their clothes, some with their boots on. Later convalescent soldiers came, French men, and as no French women were available an English resident took on the job of nurse and manager. French unmarried girls could not do nursing, but might help with meals. My sister and I undertook night duty and did alternate nights. We were alone with 30 or 40 men. Neither of us knew much about nursing but we managed somehow or other. We never saw the doctor, but got directions what to do.

In the small ward we generally had one or two very sick men, who because of high fever had to be wrapped up in icy cold cloth. The ice had to be cracked in the kitchen among the black beetles, by the light of a candle, and put in a bucket ready to soak the 2 yards of cloth. It was impossible to wring this out alone and in the process of wrapping up the man the bed was soaked. Then one had to persuade the poor fellow to swallow some vermicelli, cooked in water and tepid. Then take his temperature and wait for results.

We were expecting a new lot of men one day, and I went down to the Hospice to take over for the night. The "matrone", Mrs H., was in a hurry to get back home, to her sick mother and her 2 children. – The men have had supper – recovering from sleeping sickness – here is the paper about them. I read "One cachet [dose] each before bed. Homicidal tendancies." I did not much like this last information, and went to see the men. Only eight, each sitting beside their bed, looking the picture of misery. All had headaches. Anyhow, I thought, all of them are not likely to have these tendencies at the same time.

I gave out night shirts and when they were safely in bed took them their cachets, and left them with one small night light on the middle table. I had a small room opening out of this ward. I put the door ajar and as there was much wind that night, I tucked a chair under the handle of the door – also if anyone opened the door the chair would warn me.

I settled down and tried to read by the light of a candle, and after some time got sleepy. Suddenly there was the most frightful bang on the door, which opened sending the chair flying, and my candle blew out. Then silence. So I lit my candle and waited. One night-shirted figure appeared then 2 more, asking what had happened. A voice from a bed said he knew – a big cat, never allowed upstairs, had seen a mouse and had sprung on the mouse as it went through the crack of the door, lit by my candle. One man now caught sight of the mouse running round my room. He seized a broom and the other man a tin pail, and a chase began round and round my room, the other men cheering them on. It was a very funny sight, these 2 with bare legs and white shirts leaping about and the poor mouse trying to find a hole. All the while, to add to the noise the enormous cat had jumped onto the window sill and was howling. At last the mouse was killed, the cat jumped from the window and the men went back to bed, but all eight demanded more cachets! They were in much better spirits but said they would never sleep without more drugs. Well, I had quite explicit orders, one cachet only. I wondered if another would kill them or something. Anyhow, I gave in, and gave each another cachet as they would never have got to sleep, they had got very excited. Next morning I found them as meek as lambs and no trouble at all.

During the First World War I went often over the frontier, to Spain, to get bread and oranges, or sometimes sugar and soap. I knew several ways into Spain and the whereabouts of "ventas" as they were generally known – a farm house near the boundary, and sometimes just the hay loft in the cow shed. I could get my bicycle to within a mile or two, before taking to paths. There were both Spanish and French douaniers [customs officers] to avoid. I used to eat several oranges and a bit of bread while still in Spain, to make sure of something at least. Generally if stopped the customs man let one keep the food anyhow. If they caught sight of you it was no use running away – I enjoyed these trips very much.

I had a little Renault, a red car that was able to take 3 people, and it certainly went up to the Col de Roncevaux, which I believe is 3,600 feet. That was after the First War, in 1926. Before about 1920 there were no cars. I got a driving licence when I was just able to drive that car and turn it in the road. They asked a few questions, but as the man thought he knew English, he said we should speak in English and he did not understand my answers, so we got past that quite quickly.

In 1938 I bought a new Peugeot car, for 200 pounds. There were rumours of war, but we felt so far away in our corner of France and that the Germans would never get so far. But when France gave in the outlook was different.

In 1939 when the 2nd war began, my sister & I were both at home, in our house in Ciboure. Almost all the English residence at once left for England on a boat from Bayonne. Those who could not get on the over crowded boat, got taken off by an English cruiser waiting outside the breakwaters of the bay. We had survived the 1st war and decided to stay, thinking it unlikely that the Germans would get so far into France. Also other reasons: we had nowhere to go in England, and we had a Swiss friend living with us, also an old English friend and of course Molly! who was always a complication. We were left in peace until the unexpected capitulation of the French.

France, like Great Britain, had pursued an ambivalent policy between the wars. She maintained a numerically very large army but her air force was

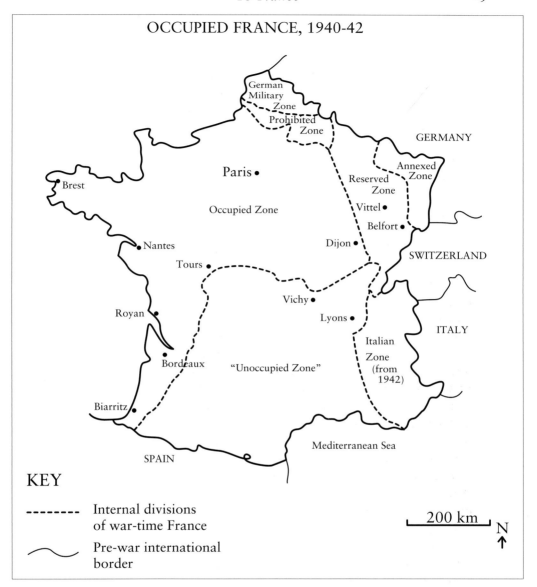

OCCUPIED FRANCE, 1940-42

German
Military
Zone

Prohibited
Zone

GERMANY

Paris •

Brest •

Reserved
Zone

Annexed
Zone

Occupied Zone

Vittel •

Belfort •

Nantes •

Dijon •

SWITZERLAND

Tours •

Vichy •

Royan •

Lyons •

ITALY

Bordeaux •

Italian
Zone
(from
1942)

"Unoccupied Zone"

Biarritz •

Mediterranean Sea

SPAIN

KEY

- - - - - - Internal divisions
of war-time France

Pre-war international
border

200 km

N
↑

weak and 'apaisement' was the watchword. In the first months of the Second
World War, France relied heavily on the defensive Maginot Line, assisted by
the troops of the British Expeditionary Force. But in May 1940, when the
might of the German war machine turned from the successful invasions
of Denmark and Norway, these defences quickly collapsed. Holland and
Belgium were over-run in a matter of days, and the Expeditionary Force,
together with a contingent of 113,000 French troops, was evacuated from
Dunkirk and elsewhere in the week beginning 25 May.

On 14 June, the Germans reached Paris, where they found that the French Government had already left, heading for Bordeaux. The Prime Minister argued for continued resistance, but he was outvoted. He was replaced by the elderly First World War hero, Marshal Pétain, a right-wing authoritarian who negotiated an armistice with Germany.

Meanwhile, the German Panzers swept on, supported by the all-powerful Luftwaffe, simply bypassing areas of significant French resistance. They encircled a large part of the French Army north of Belfort in mid-June, and reached the western naval port of Brest on the 19th. The Loire was crossed at Nantes on 20th, by which time the invaders were also already at Lyons, far to the south-east. They reached the Gironde at Royan on 24 June, the day the armistice was concluded. At the last minute, Italy declared war on France on 21 June and invaded over the alpine border, but was repulsed by a heavily outnumbered unit of French troops.

Under the terms of the German-French armistice, Hitler allowed Italy to occupy the south-east of France, from the Mediterranean to Lake Geneva, while Germany occupied the whole of the north, together with the entire Atlantic coast down to the Spanish border. The north-east was divided into several smaller regions: some were annexed to Germany; others were under strict military control. Almost 1,850,000 French prisoners from these areas were left in German hands, of whom one and a half million were put to work as forced labourers of various sorts; fewer than a million of these survived the war. Meanwhile, the unoccupied portion of France left in the middle was ruled from Vichy, by Marshal Pétain.

Of the twenty-four clauses in the armistice, some were of immediate practical value to the victors, others perhaps seem more sinister with hindsight. All troops beyond those needed for internal security were to be disarmed, and all military hardware was to be handed over. German nationals resident in France were to be given up to the Reich on request and all government procedures were to conform to German practices. One and a half million political prisoners were taken to Germany as hostages, and France had to agree to the transport of 'merchandise in transit' over the non-occupied zone. In exchange, Germany undertook merely 'to take into account what is necessary for the life of those living in the non-occupied territories'.

The speed at which these events occurred took everyone by surprise, not least the expatriate community.

When France gave in, the Germans were very quickly all over France. One day we were warned that they were already in Guethary [on the coast, well south of Biarritz], only a few miles away, everyone to stay indoors & no cars on the roads. Being English I knew they would take my nearly new car so I got it out & went down our road. In order to get to a garage I had to cross the Route Nationale [the main N10 road from Biarritz into Spain] to get on the right side. I was ½ across when I saw the German army close by. Trucks & cars, gun carriages etc., men standing up in them singing and shouting. They had passed St Jean & were on their way to the frontier. They could not stop the whole lot for me, luckily, so I got as far into the gutter as I could, and got past a great many of them, and got to the garage.

At the garage, where of course I was well known, I told them take off my name & all signs of English & sell it or keep it or do anything you like with it, only don't let <u>them</u> have it. They sold it that evening and I think they got 100 pounds and it was got over the frontier. So that was how I got rid of my car, unfortunately. To get back home I had to cross the Route Nationale again – I was helped by the garage & I got home by a smugglers path which came out near our house. There was a continuous stream of Germans, going down to the frontier. That was the beginning.

Almost at once 2 plain clothed Germans walked in to the house & took our very old radio, a great loss to us. It was too big to hide. When we protested one opened his coat to show 'Gestapo'. They demanded field glasses. Luckily we had forseen this & I had hidden my very good glasses under one of the beehives, just where the bees went in and out, and got well stung in the process. The glasses stayed there during the war & were none the worse. Our 2 bicycles were hidden in the garden.

German soldiers often walked in, asking the same questions, over and over again, and we had to report to them in St Jean every week. We had to go and report every day or every few days, we were not allowed to go out far.

We had an English friend with French nationality & I went to listen to the English news chez elle. She was caught one day while listening to England, she was alone and confessed it was England. The German was very decent and told her she should have denied it. After that we were more careful and one of us kept a look out. We put clothes over our heads and kept the radio very quiet. Later, this friend was sent into "the unoccupied".

The first few days after the coming of the Germans were, for my sister and me the most worrying of the whole duration. Molly by this time was over 50 & could not walk owing to her hip. She did not get downstairs at all.

My sister and I and our English friend were all taken up one day & driven to an hotel in St Jean. There we were locked in a bedroom. By looking out of the window we could talk to other perplexed people. We were there for a week. I was taken home the first day, in a jeep to get some things for the night & a German came to each room and looked at everything I collected.

The hotel fed us well and friends American and French collected outside and talked to us as we could get on to the roof of the hotel. We heard afterwards it was because Hitler was passing by rail to see Franco in Spain.

After this we were left alone for a while.

3

The Knock on the Door

At the start of December 1940, as the worst winter in living memory bit
deep into Europe, the Reich began rounding up the women in the occupied zone who held British papers. Some, like Aunt Fan and her sisters,
were expatriates who had chosen to remain when others were evacuated.
Others had more tenuous connections to Britain: some had merely been
born there because of their father's job. A few, normally resident in Britain,
were temporarily in France at the outbreak of hostilities, on holiday, or on
business or visiting relations. Many had British husbands or fathers, perhaps 'tommies' from the Great War. They were a diverse group culturally
and socially, from stable boys' wives to Indian royalty.

Both Aunt Fan's parents had died shortly before the Second War began,
and she and her older sister Kathleen, themselves in late middle age, were
living in the house which their father had built above St Jean-de-Luz,
looking after their handicapped sister Molly. The weather was already
unseasonably cold in Ciboure, where winter temperatures normally
remained above freezing, when the Twemlow sisters had warning that
they were to be taken away, as Aunt Fan later described in her notebooks:

Early in Dec 1940, we got a message from the American consul in
Biarritz. He sent one of his secretaries, a French girl, round at night to
say that we were going to be taken to Germany the next day, my sisters
and I, and we must be ready. He advised us to take no food, and only the
clothes we could carry. So friends came round, and two friends lent us
big cloaks – it was a very cold winter.

We asked for a Doctor to come & see Molly. A very smart young man
came, spoke English, brand new uniform. We kept Molly in bed & told
her to say her leg was very bad. It was true as she had had a fall. He came
to the open door & Molly pointed to him & said loudly "Who is this

Boy?" We were dismayed, so I think was he as without going further he said "certainly she can stay".

The next day came the expected knock on the door:

We put on extra clothes – 2 skirts, 2 pairs of stockings, 2 of everything we could. And then we packed our small suitcases with just what we could carry. Our English friend who was 74, & of course the Swiss, were allowed to stay in the house, with our faithful Basque maid Myiti.

We were in fairly good spirits, because we had been taken up before, when Hitler came to see Franco, and we had been kept in an hotel for 2 or 3 days. We were quite comfortable. So we thought we'd be quite comfortable somewhere else.

Next day was my birthday.

The Germans came and took us to the station, and we were put into third class carriages, with other people from St Jean and round about. We had a young mother with 2 children – the father was French and this was a sort of second family he had. We had no food with us. At one station they were selling sandwiches and some people got a sandwich or something, but it was all used up before they got to our carriage.

We made fairly good friends with the German guard, and when he was walking outside in the corridor, and the train was going slowly just outside a station, we wrote notes and wrapped them up with a 5 franc piece, and leaning out of the window we dropped them for the workmen who were standing aside to let the train go by, in the hopes that the notes would get home. One or two did arrive – we heard afterwards that they got them. But of course it was rather risky. The German guard never spotted it, fortunately.

Well, we were all night in the train. It was heated at first, but we had had nothing to eat. Then we were shunted into a siding, and while we were there the heating went off, and we were very cold. It was snowing hard. Then we went on again.

They brought tins, one per compartment. But we couldn't open it. The German guard managed to get it open with his bayonet and it was full of white lard. We were also given a very mouldy bit of German bread. We didn't eat very much of that.

We went on, and at Angouleme they stopped the train again and we all got out and crossed a yard and went into a room where there were trestles, and we were given small washbasins like a large bowl of very good, hot pea soup. It was the Red Cross gave it to us. Well, we most of us finished our whole bowl of that stuff and I must say we were glad of it. And then we went back to the train, and it was snowing and freezing,

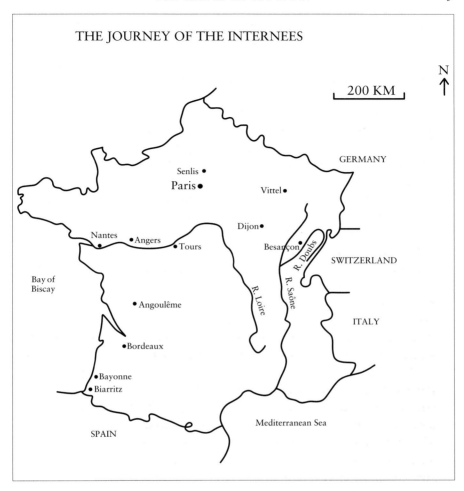

THE JOURNEY OF THE INTERNEES

200 KM

N

GERMANY

Senlis •
Paris •

Vittel •

Dijon •

Besançon •

SWITZERLAND

R. Doubs

R. Saône

R. Loire

Nantes •
• Angers
• Tours

Bay of
Biscay

• Angoulême

ITALY

• Bordeaux

• Bayonne
• Biarritz

Mediterranean Sea

SPAIN

terrible weather. We spent another night and day in the train – we were
eating our lard by then! And then we arrived at Besançon.

All over the occupied zone, the same orders had gone out, and women
and small children were being taken to police stations, town halls, schools
and barracks. The initial round-up was clearly organised with military
precision, but as the Twemlow sisters discovered, the process thereafter
descended into something closer to chaos. It seems to have mattered much
more to the occupying Germans that their prisoners should have no warning of their departure, minimising any chance of escape, and all arrive
together, than for any preparations for food and comfort be made for the
journey. Without the intervention of the Red Cross, even at this early stage,
conditions for the internees would have been much worse.

The accounts of some of the people involved tell their own personal stories, united by the bitter cold, hunger and complete ignorance of their destination.

Sister Patricia McGauley, a young nun of the Congregation of La Retraite, was arrested and held in detention in Angers before being sent away. She was warned in advance by her superiors that she was going to be interned, and so was able to take some food and a blanket with her. She and another sister from her convent were held in Angers barracks for three days, with eight nuns of other Orders, while more British subjects were rounded up. Then they were given rations for four days, and escorted to the station:

After three days in the barracks in Angers, Sister Mary Catherine and I were taken by train to Besançon to the most inhuman conditions possible. It was on December 5th that we were taken away. We were all ten put into one carriage with only a short corridor and toilet. The communicating door was locked so we were completely separated from everybody else. Barbed wire was fixed onto the outside handles of the doors. We had no idea of our destination but seemed to zigzag all over France picking up more British subjects each time we stopped.

We shared our provisions of bread, cheese and paté and longed for something to drink. One of the Sisters had a bottle of Eau de Cologne with which we managed to refresh ourselves a little until the little old Nazareth nun managed to spill the lot.

But on one occasion somebody passed through the window a small bowl of water into which ten pairs of hands splashed it up into our faces. Once or twice we were handed in a drink but the train started to pull out before it had scarcely touched our lips … and the people on the platform were clamouring for their cups.

One day a German soldier came to see us. He showed us his Rosary and said that he didn't want this war any more than we did. All he wanted was to go home to his wife and children. He had been told that we were going to a hospital and I think that he genuinely believed that to be true.

[On the] Tuesday night we were left in the station in Besançon and in the morning there were signs of movement outside. Covered wagons were on the platform and the barbed wire was being removed from the doors. A soldier stopped me in my eagerness to get out, whilst Sister Mary Catherine reminded me that his gun was loaded! We were again lifted in covered wagons and driven to our next destination where we were given our orders by a fair haired, blue eyed young man who spoke with a perfect Oxford accent. He was just wearing the wrong uniform!

It was snowing when we arrived.

William Webb, an English boy whose family lived and worked just north of Paris, was thirteen in 1940. His father had already been arrested and interned some weeks previously, but William was considered too young. Then in December, German soldiers came to the house with orders that his mother and older sister, too, should pack. This time, William was too old according to the German regulations, and so was not permitted to go with them; only small children and old men were to accompany the women to their camp. So he was to be left behind. A German sentry was left to guard them until the transport returned:

The sentry stood rigidly in the gateway and prevented Mother from going onto the pavement.

The hour had long passed. We vainly hoped the order was cancelled? George was back at the shutter and told us all English people were arrested and waiting to be picked up. No one knew where the women were to be taken. We had some bread and jam for lunch ...

Ready by the doorway, were the two small suitcases with two thick coats and folded blankets with Mother's grey shawl above them. A black canvas bag held some food, mostly bread and jam, that was all we had. Mother hugged me and we cried our eyes out ...

Outside, sleet was falling. The guard paced up and down the yard, obviously cold ... It was mid afternoon and already the light was failing. The sound of approaching traffic was heard. A car stopped outside the gate followed by an open sided truck. Soldiers were tramping the pavement as they responded to orders.

An officer came to the door. "Frau Webb und Fraulein Beatrix, Komen mit mir" [*Come with me*]. A Feldwebel behind him was more direct "Rous und schnell, Komen schnell" [*Get a move on*], he barked. Mother had not responded quickly enough to his command, so he entered the kitchen and shoved her along. I stood in the room shaking with fear. Six armed soldiers stood in the small yard and formed a lane between which we walked ... George and Mme Menetre came and held my hands ... The officer ordered Mother and Beatrix into the truck, the back board was lowered and Beatrix clambered into it, but it was impossible for Mother to negotiate it and she insisted a step be provided. Other English women, some with children filled the truck. They were sitting on benches along the inside of the lorry. The Germans were in a hurry, the whole process had taken far too long and the officers were getting irritated.

Nellie Chambers, our head lad's wife, was in the lorry. Nellie was a fearless loud-mouthed person. As the Germans searched for a step for Mother, she saw me crying and shouted at the top of her voice "Pleur pas Willy. Ils sont foutus les sales Boches! Bandes des Salauds! C'est des

Fumiers! Cochon de Boches!" [*Don't cry, Willy. The filthy Boches are done for! Bunch of bastards! They're a pile of crap! German pigs!*] raising her fist at the officers. "Ils sont finites maintenant qu'ils attaques les femmes". [*They're finished! Now they're reduced to attacking women!*]. She did not stop her banter. The embarrassed Germans had no answer to her flow of language. Over a dozen French people had congregated around the lorry and watched proceedings. The officers were livid. Finally, a small drum was found and it enabled Mother to get into the truck. The tail board was raised, two armed soldiers joined the women in the back and the officer waved and the lorry was gone within seconds. Nellie spat at the officer as a parting gesture.

I can still see that truck vanishing around the back of the church, with Mother waving bravely. I stood rooted to the pavement, Mme Menetre was crying as she held me in her arms. George was stunned and took us into his warm house. "Where have they taken them?" I asked. George was angry. "I shall go to the Kommandatur and find out tomorrow morning. Bande de Salauds."

Father knew something was taking place as [his] camp was a hotbed of rumours. The men were very bitter that the women and children had been picked up. The rumour was that this was Hitler's revenge at Britain's refusal to surrender and for having defeated the Luftwaffe. The internees were in a state of uproar. A camp delegation was being formed to petition the camp Kommandant to have the wives and children released ... Guards at the camp had been increased as trouble was anticipated: men expecting a visit from their wives were very angry and demonstrated.

When his mother was eventually released from the camps, she told William what had happened next:

After three days in Senlis Barracks [north of Paris], all ambulatory persons were made to walk to the station, [Mother] carrying our suitcase and blanket. The only exceptions were the stretcher cases who stayed behind and were eventually released. On the platform a train, made up of old third class wooden carriages fitted with wooden slatted benches, awaited their arrival. Armed soldiers detailed eight women into each compartment and locked them in. Mother made sure Auntie was with her. They were not told where they were being taken to when the unheated train moved off without any electric lighting. The cold was intense. The carriages had no corridors and to relieve themselves Mother devised a method whereby a toilet bag was used as a container and the contents poured out of the window. The journey to Besançon, for that was their destination, took three days. On one occasion the train stopped in open country and the prisoners were allowed to climb down onto the track to 'do their business' in front of everyone; including the guards who thought it a great joke. During the first night, soldiers distributed a boulle [small loaf or a roll] of black bread to be shared by two people. This was their first food, no refreshments were given. Slowly the train lurched on with its cargo of cold, parched and starving prisoners. During the second night the train briefly stopped at an unlit station and the women were allowed out; they rushed to the toilets but many relieved themselves on the platform. During that day, at another station, German Schwesters (nurses) handed out ersatz coffee. The cold was so intense that they huddled together in an attempt to keep warm. Besançon was reached at 4.30 am on the fourth day, it was dark and snowing. After being herded in open trucks they were assembled in a large covered building which was the riding ring of the Vauban Barracks.

Rita Muller (née Harding) was aged eighteen in 1940. She had lived in France since she was a small child, when her father went to work for an American bank in Paris. By the outbreak of war, her parents were divorced, and her father had remarried, but the two families remained on friendly terms. Her father and his second wife, who was Jewish, moved out of Paris into the area which later became the unoccupied zone and – although this was kept secret at the time – became involved in the Resistance. Later on in the war, when the Germans took over Vichy France, Mr Harding was rounded up with many others, and sent to the internment camp at St Denis, near Paris; by then his Jewish wife was also of course in great danger. When France was liberated he was repatriated to England as quickly as possible. Meanwhile, Rita, with her mother and two sisters, had decided to move to the north Biscay coast early in 1940, in the hope of avoiding the conflict. Like so many people, they could not imagine that the war would ever spread so far. After the German-French Armistice, however, they found themselves in the occupied zone:

Rita Harding (left) at the Vittel camp, where she worked in the hospital.

At first all was well but by October 1940 the Germans threatened the French with death if they harboured English nationals and didn't report them.

From October we had to go to the German Kommandatur every day to sign on and show ourselves. On December 5th early in the morning German soldiers came to arrest us. After a few days spent in a school, sleeping on the floor, we were taken to Nantes, with the other English picked up in the Vendée and boarded a train for 6 days and nights, sitting in 3rd class wooden carriages on wooden seats, with no heating (it was December). We were locked in the carriages, of course. At the end of that journey we arrived in Besançon ... and walked to the ghastly Caserne Vauban where we were kept for five months.

A New Zealander and his Scottish wife, Samuel and Elizabeth Hales, had tried to escape to England when they realised that the Germans were coming. Samuel was then seventy-two and Elizabeth sixty-three. They were both professional artists, and had originally moved to Paris at the turn of the century to further their training. There they had met and married, and both had exhibited at the Paris Salon, while Samuel also ran the Paris American Art Shop for artists' materials. In the summer of 1940, the Hales' joined the great exodus of fleeing people on the last train for Brittany; a train that was twice halted and attacked by German aeroplanes, which gunned down the terrified refugees as they tried to take shelter. When they eventually reached the coast, they discovered that the last boat had sailed and the Germans had got there ahead of them, so they were forced to return to Paris. There the Hales' were soon denounced to the Gestapo by a neighbour who thought they had a radio transmitter in their flat. After this, they were left in relative peace until their arrest.

Elizabeth Hales kept pencil notes during her time as an internee at Besançon, and made a fair copy of them, although leaving much of it in note form, soon after her release. It may be no coincidence that it was the older prisoners, like Aunt Fan and Mrs Hales, who tried to keep diaries of life in the camps; perhaps they were more aware of the significance of the events they were caught up in. Elizabeth Hales subsequently extended her account of the internment into a diary of daily life in Paris during the occupation. This final version is now in the possession of her grandson:

Samuel Hales, aged 72 at the time of his arrest.

Early on morning of December 5th 1940 a tap came to my bedroom door and the concierge's voice said, 'Madame I have bad news to announce. The police have come to arrest you and Mr Hales.' I dashed out of bed began dressing myself and soon afterwards reached the drawing room where I saw Sam dressing and a Paris policeman sitting beside him. Said he, 'in half an hour you must be dressed to go with me to the Mairie [Town Hall].' Half dazed I started to dress fully and to collect my things. The concierge went down stairs again …

We filled a sack with clothes and food stuffs were put into a suit case. The police grumbled and said I was slow but when I gave him half a pound of coffee he became sweet and said if questioned he would say I was out when he called and had to wait on me. My jewels and some dresses went into Mme Faugeras's safe keeping. Meanwhile we ate a hurried breakfast and I put on my best things fur coat etc and good hat – very warm things as police said we were going to a very cold place …

We moved towards police court in Mairie of 14th arrondissement [urban district] and there found a great hubbub. All the Paris police seemed concentrated there. It was goodbye to wee Miss F. and we entered into the hall to present our passports to the police. Notes being taken of us. There we climbed upstairs to the sale du marriages [chamber for the registration of civil marriages] a lovely room with frises of young couples in bridal dress. The room was filled with British people, many my friends …

On platform were several German officers with registers open before them, in which they entered our names. There we sat while the morning fled away. Our hand baggage with labels attached was at further end of hall. Finally a German officer came forward and said 6 young people could go out and seek provisions. It was now 12 o'clock. My German was of use to me. I said to officer, 'can't I go too?' And he replied, 'Yes, if you go quick.' So down I went with active young policeman and a girl. Said the police 'all the sorties were suppressed last night and the police sent out to arrest all British subjects in Paris' 'pray God les anglais may gain' (By which I suppose he meant that the roads out of Paris had been barricaded, and that he prayed for an Allied victory). Meanwhile we hastened along and bought our goods – butter sausages bread. Soon the quarter of an hour was up and we entered the Mairie again. And there we sat till 3 pm. Then came orders from German officers that we must go downstairs again. At door we found several buses awaiting us. Sam, Mrs Cox and I were soon bundled into a bus along with 7 other people, flanked by police always …

Trains awaited us, three soon being filled up. And there we sat for hours. Later soup was handed round by German red cross nurses. It was good and made one feel better. Evening came on, and at 8 we slowly left Paris. For a time we hoped we were going to suburbs but as time wore on we began to see that we were going some distance away – evidently east and we wondered where. In the darkness we distinguished various stations. In due time we reached Troyes where we rested for a time. In every station we saw Germans. Occasionally they handed us hot drinks and once a tin of meat – a kind of sausage. we stopped some time at Troyes. Some people say we were moving on to Frankfurt-on-Mein or Poland but were stopped by American embassy and diverted towards Besancon. ...

Evening drew on and we quite enjoyed the landscape. Finally at 5 pm the 3 trains drew up and before us we saw a big sign-post with Besancon printed on it. It all seemed a dream, we saw before us a crowd of German soldiers with carriages and small Prussian horses. Some ambulance red cross carriages too. Gradually we all stepped out. The younger people were put in groups and made to walk up to the caserne [barracks] while Sam and older folks were bundled into vans and driven about a mile up to caserne.

Miss Mabel Bayliss had remained at her home in Paris after the outbreak of war. She was rounded up on the same day as Aunt Fan, but with much less warning, and no inkling that it was to be for more than a few hours:

In abiding by regulations and signing at the local police station every day, we imagined our liberty was to continue. Alas! on December 5th, 1940, at a quarter to eight in the morning there was a ring at my door. It was dark, there was still a complete black-out. I opened the door and a huge policeman brandished his torch on me. "Miss B.", he said, "I have come to fetch you". I was horrified and asked what I had done. He stalked into my flat. He told me not to be upset, to take my bath, and have my breakfast calmly, then go with him; that I had three quarters of an hour to get ready. He strutted about my flat, then his gaze rested upon my books. I wondered if he had seen anything of which he disapproved. He examined some insignificant typescript, then went to the kitchen and burnt it. This I imagine he did to help me; I thought it warranted a drink. In spite of the early hour he was delighted to accept. Seeing some port given to me by American friends (the first time I have seen or drunk this wine in France), he nodded to it; I just seized an ordinary tumbler and gave him some; am afraid I was too liberal with the quantity. I went out and hurriedly dressed ... Thinking that maybe I was going to be kept at the police station during a thorough inspection of my flat, the policeman told me to wear a warm coat and take a rug for fear I stayed the night. I took my smallest valise and no clothes to change into.

Not until arriving at the Town Hall and perceiving the mass of people did I realise that the Germans were rounding us up.

Such an agglomeration of people at the Town Hall! Just our names were noted. We were led into the court-yard, and there closed lorries and police vans were waiting for us; as soon as one vehicle was full, it started off, to be followed by a stream of others. As far as possible we were hidden from the public gaze but some French people looked curiously at us. On one side of me I had a young Jewish girl and on the other a French woman, who could not say a word of English. Having married a Britisher many years ago and been a widow for over 30 years, she could not understand why she was arrested with Britishers. We were driven to the Gare de l'Est; there, an extremely long train was waiting for us. We were hurriedly bundled into the carriages, then the doors were locked. None of the people I had come with were in my carriage. We tried to be gay and turned everything into a comedy, but later, one of my fellow travellers with spinal trouble, having been bedridden for many years, became alarmingly ill and lay flat on the floor. This person, from the moment we arrived at Besançon, I never saw again. In the next compartment was a young mother with her tiny baby. The latter persisted in screaming, and as time went on the mother also copiously wept. She begged for milk for her child. The German told her she must wait until the next morning. This young woman and child I also never saw again.

The long dreary day the train remained stationary at the station. We were given some black bread and a tin of what we called 'Monkey'. What it was none of us knew; the smell and appearance of this uncooked meat I shall never forget. In spite of feeling ready for a meal we could not tackle it and the tin of meat was eventually thrown out of the window.

Whilst we travelled during the night anxiety prevented any sleep, even if the crying baby, sighs and groans had not done so. The following afternoon the train slowed up into a railway siding and there we were greeted by a file of sentries standing at attention. A mass of women, many aged and many ill, so much so that many were unable to walk and were packed into barrack carts with their valises. It was a dreary, cold, muddy day. We trudged along. Among the crowd, to my joy, I discovered a friend …

Mrs Sofka Skipwith had only recently arrived in France from London. She was a highly educated Russian émigré from a senior aristocratic family, recently married to an Englishman. She had gone to Paris in April, leaving her three young sons (two by her first marriage) in England, to visit her mother and other members of the Russian community there, and in the hope of seeing her husband while he was on leave from the RAF.

Sofka Skipwith, her husband Grey and their baby son, just before the outbreak of war.

On 9 August she heard that British men were being interned, and by the end of the month British women were being required to register daily at the Commissariat. On 16 October a new decree was issued in Paris that anyone harbouring a British subject must declare their presence by the 20th, or they would be shot:

On the morning of 7th [December] came a knock on my door. A gendarme. "I must ask you to come with me. Take things for 24 hours". It turned out to be a round-up of all British women.

We sat in a room at the police station until, late in the afternoon, the place was filled with Germans. We were herded into open trucks: "Los! Los! Raus!" [Move! Move! Out!] A cold drive across Paris to the Gare de L'Est, nostalgically staring at the familiar streets. We were rammed and jostled into a waiting train. It moved off. We had no idea of our destination.

Collect a train load of people, herd them together without any information as to where they were being taken and in no time you will have 'authoritative rumours', 'bobards' the French call them. They swept through the train: we were being taken to Germany as slave labour; we were about to be repatriated; we were being transferred to the unoccupied zone of France. Some three days later we found ourselves in Besançon, in newly emptied barracks.

Annie Strong (née Luks) was just ten years old when she, her mother and her little sister Francine, aged three, had their visit from the authorities at Ivry-sur-Seine, on the southern outskirts of Paris:

> How well I remember that morning when a German soldier and a French policeman came knocking at the door of our apartment in Ivry. No details were given to my mother except that she, as a British subject, with her two daughters were to be escorted to the Mairie in Ivry. Just a formality, the French policeman said, you will be back home later in the day, so don't bother to take anything with you.
>
> My Aunt, as well as my Grandmother, who both worked in different sections of the Mairie, found out what had happened. My Aunt raced to the apartment in a frantic state, for she had been told that we were to be taken to a camp in Germany. As we were escorted, my mother, sister Francine and I to the Mairie, with all the neighbours silently watching, my aunt collected whatever she could in the way of warm clothes for us, as it was early December. She arrived just in time to give my mother a couple of bags before we were taken away in buses towards the Gare De l'Est. Some others were not so fortunate. One mother from nearby Ivry Fort had two young children as well as a very sick young baby. She was not able to pack anything.
>
> At the Gare De l'Est we were again herded into a long train together with hundreds of British subjects from all over Paris, mostly women, children and elderly people. The younger husbands, fathers and sons (over the age of 19) had already been taken away a few days earlier. The train was packed – without heating – or supplies of food. We were not told where we were going. It was cold, in our compartment, and the poor little sick baby coughed all the time. After such a long time the train stopped. Looking out all we could see was heavy snow and a line of German soldiers along the platform. It terrified my sister who started to scream. That scene will always stay in my mind. We didn't know where we were but eventually we were told that the place was Besançon, in the Jura. We would be accommodated in old barracks called Vauban.
>
> It transpired the next day that the Germans had decided to take us all to a concentration camp in Germany. The Red Cross who, apparently, had a lot of sway in the early days of the occupation of France, told the Germans that they could not take mothers with their children and the elderly into Germany, hence our unexpected and unprepared stop in Besançon.

The Gumuchian family, by contrast, were of Armenian extraction and originally from Turkey. The parents had moved to England early in the century and so escaped the massacres, and they had settled in Manchester where they took British citizenship. There they had met and married, and had moved to the Continent in 1921, at which time their younger daughter Sonia was five years old. Sonia is still living in Paris, and vividly remembers the conditions in the camps, and the day the knock came on their door:

> My father died in 1936, and after that we had no reason to return to England because Stella and I had already started to work.
>
> We were arrested on December 5th 1940 and, being from Paris, were with the first ones to arrive in Besançon on the 6th, on a cold and rainy day in a 'Vauban Palace', dirty and empty.

Fernande Oldfield (née Bugnano) was a couturier in her early twenties who held British papers because her Italian father had been working in London at the time of her birth. She trained with Norman Hartnell there, but had recently moved back to her mother's village near Versailles:

Fernande Oldfield at Besançon.

It was on the 5th of December 1940 that a military policeman from the German army, accompanied by a French policeman, banged on the door and burst into my house, telling me to prepare for a 'check on my papers' for which I should take a change of clothes and one blanket, and that he would come back for me later. He left, but the French policeman was left to keep watch on me.

He was a young man, not much older than me, married and with a child of a few months. He lived in Versailles and had been woken at 5 am to go with the military policeman. His first words were 'above all do not run away because they would shoot me'. He went with me to the village post office to buy stamps and to say goodbye to my aunt and uncle.

After lunch, the German returned. The farewell to my parents was tearful but without looking back I got into a bus already containing many British.

Our first stop was at the Château Mesnil St Denis to pick up a Scottish lady and there we were given a generous tea (tea, cocoa and little cakes) by the proprietor. Our second stop was to search an enclosed convent for a Canadian sister of 50. She had been there since the age of six. Next we picked up a mother and her two children, but when the German saw this woman coming unsteadily, a newborn baby of barely two days in her arms and the other little one clutching her coat-tails, he signalled to her to stop and said 'go back to the house'. He must have been a father himself to break his orders in this way.

We rejoined the road and reached the railway station at Maison Lafitte at the end of the afternoon. There we got into a train and they handed out bread and a bit of jam and then we were off. The train went very slowly and evening came and we slept. Waking with a start, it was 5 am (6th December) at Versailles railway station. After a long stop, the train set off again and it wasn't until the afternoon that we reached Villeneuve St Georges [only about 35 km from Versailles by train]. There again we were held up for a long time. Rumours were circulated that the American Ambassador had intervened here, with the result that we were not deported to Germany. It was not in fact the Americans but the British Government, by the mediation of the French Red Cross, which indicated to the Germans that if they deported British subjects to Germany, Britain would deport all German prisoners to Canada.

Again a departure, and it was not until 7th December, at 6 am, that we arrived at Besançon. Two military lorries were waiting for us and took us to the courtyard of the 60th Regiment of Infantry at Caserne Vauban, which became for us Frontstalag 142.

All was dreary, and it was terribly cold.

4

Aunt Fan's Diary

While she was interned, Aunt Fan not only kept a diary, but she made numerous sketches, using whatever paper she could find. Many of these original illustrations survive, having been smuggled out of the camps at various times. These are on an assortment of pieces of paper, the earliest ones being no more than tiny scraps of whatever she could lay her hands on. After she had been at the Besançon camp for some time, she managed to obtain a pad of proper drawing paper and some pencils and colours, as she remembered later with immense delight. Thereafter, the quality of the work improves. After her release she made a fair copy of the diary together with a selection of the pictures, which she bound and covered with scenes from the camps. At first the diary seems to have been written regularly, but later on it only records the major events in camp life. Her spelling, as ever, is decidedly idiosyncratic and she cheerfully uses a French word when the English one eludes her.

Dec 5ᵗʰ In the morning at nine o'clock two German soldiers came and told us to be ready to leave at 11o'c. One man sat down in the hall and the other went to fetch a German doctor. The doctor came and after seeing Molly gave permission for her to stay in the charge of our maid.

Several friends came and between talking to them, packing and getting a few valuables out of the house under the nose of the sentinel, the three hours passed quickly.

We were to take warm clothes, but only what we could carry ourselves. Kathleen and I could each carry our two valises but we could only allow ourselves one book each – a small Shakespeare and Emma. We wore our heaviest clothes and a friend lent us each a big cloak.

We were taken by car to the Hotel Edward VII, where we had been shut up once before for three days. We had a fairly good lunch and then were interviewed by German officers. Our friend of 74 years old was allowed to go home to look after Molly on condition that she did not leave the house and garden.

We sat about not knowing what was to be our fate till at 6.30 when two big auto cars arrived and we were taken to Bayonne station. French porters at the station were willing to help us as some people could not carry their baggage, but they were told to stand back – Between us we got to the train and then waited for two hours in third class carriages, unlighted and unheated. The train was very long and already had a big contingent from Biarritz and Bayonne. We were given loaves of German bread and a large tin of pâté or of lard one between 3 of us and a tin of sardines each. This we were told was food for four days. The bread was heavy stodgy stuff almost impossible to disintegrate with penknives and the loaves were mostly intact at the end of the journey.

We were four in a carriage with two soldiers to guard us in the end compartment. These men continually walked along the corridor in order to count us by means of a flashlight – None of us had any idea of escaping and fortunately none of us had any idea that we were going to be three days and three nights bottled up in that train. The train was very long and there were several hundred other English in the rest of the train.

About 9 o'c we started, the train still unheated and stopping continually for long periods, till at last we got to Bordeaux at 2.30 in the morning.

Dec 6th There we waited, sometimes shunted, expecting every minute to go on – The hours of waiting seemed endless and it was not till 2.15 in the afternoon that we started again. We had eaten a little of the bread and tried the pâté which was not bad. The soldiers cut the bread for us and opened the tins with their bayonettes. In Bordeaux we were told to remain seated when trains passed and not to appear at the windows.

We had three small children among our party, and in Bordeaux some German officers and Red + nurses arrived and called for the children to come to the door of the compartment – There they were given a drink of milk and the whole scene was photographed by a German in uniform.

We got some water before leaving Bordeaux but had only our rubber hot water bottles to keep it in. We had no cups but two thermos tops between us all.

At 5.30 we arrived at Angouleme. Here we were told to get out of the train, leaving all our luggage in the carriage. It was very cold and raining. Several hundred of us were marshalled across a road into a big shed set with benches and tables. We were a miserable looking crowd of children middle aged and very old people, mostly women. We were quickly served each with a small washing basin of hot thick pea soup. This we were very glad of although the basins reminded one rather too much of channel crossings. When we came out it was snowing and we saw two other sad processions of men – many of them coloured men looking perished in inadequate garments. We had great difficulty in finding our carriage the train was so long and everybody's baggage looking alike. We were sorted at last. By this time we were pretty sure we were going to the N.E. – Nancy or Belfort it was thought. We left Angouleme at about six o'clock and got to Tours at 5.30 next morning.

Dec 7th In the station we bought dates and ham sandwiches without leaving the train. There were not nearly enough for everybody – No heating all night and we were very cold. It was our second night in the train.

There was only one man in our coach, he was old but uncomplaining. The first night he sat up all the time but the second he was so frozen that the three women with him put him to bed on one side wrapped up in shawls and newspapers. He was very grateful and amused them most of the night with funny stories and even operatic airs. We all spent a cold and miserable night.

At Tours we stayed an interminable time, from 5.30 till mid day. Then we started in an easternly direction – We travelled all night but could not see the name of any station except that of Bourges.

Dec 8th The train was at last heated. Outside it was snowing – At about 8 o'c on Sunday morning we arrived at Besançon – it was bitter as when the train stopped the heating stopped and it was still snowing hard.

French prisoners were on the platform ready to help with our baggage and to carry some of the old people on stretchers to the waiting army ambulances – Many people were taken straight to a big hospital in the town. The rest of us were driven off in closed vans and deposited in a big empty garage – We stood about very tired and cold having had no sort of breakfast and trying not to lose sight of each other or of our baggage.

Presently we were marshalled out into a yard and directed to three big barrack buildings. We found ours, Batiment "C" indescribably dirty, and the other two were just the same. All one side of the building was one big rubbish heap and inside old straw mattresses in all stages of decay on the floor, old shoes, helmets and soldiers discarded rags and dirt everywhere.

We quickly took possession of a big room, "we" being 14 of us all from St Jean or near by, threw out the rags etc and searched in other rooms for cleaner sacks of straw until we had collected 14 of them. All this time we

'Caserne Vauban.'

had had nothing to eat. We were feeling utterly dismayed at the state of the building prepared for us. None of us had had a proper meal or any sleep to speak of for 3 days and nights. Still none of us collapsed.

We found that others were queuing up outside a building for soup. Two of us went but we had nothing to get the soup in "Get something off the rubbish heap" we were told – "any old tin or even a helmet." We hunted over the smelly heap and at last with the help of a kindly old man, found a big gamelle [mess tin] without holes. We took it to a tap and with earth and our hands cleaned it as well as we could. Then after a long wait lined up in the snow we got it filled with soup and potatoes and were also given 14 spoons. We put the tin in the middle of the table and all dipped in our spoons. It was 4 days before we had plates – but slices of German bread made quite good plates to eat the potatoes.

During the meal the eldest of our party quietly collapsed on to her sack of straw and there she remained too weak to move for 3 days. A young French doctor came at once. There were six French doctors at the Infirmary all prisoners like ourselves and very friendly and sympathetic.

By the evening we had gathered 14 beds of sorts, rough wooden frames with planks or wire to hold the sack of straw. The sacks were made of very good strong linen. No sort of pillow. We were given 2 brown

'View from our window.'

blankets each, two basins for the lot of us 2 cans and a big pail. We washed in turn on the only table.

Soldiers fixed up a stove for us early in the afternoon – It was a god-send as it burnt well. Other rooms were smoked out by their stoves. Wood and coal was lying about all over the place. Supper was of brown sweet tisane [an infusion made with barley] and bread. We fetched it in our only can and were given a cup each. None of us slept much that night on our unfamiliar beds and our heads on bundles of clothes or suitcases.

Our room was very big, 20 yards long and on the 2nd story. The floor was cement. We had 56 stone steps to come up and the water taps were on the ground floor, in a big washing room fitted with troughs and icy cold water. There was one lavatory in the building for every two or three hundred people – it was a hole in the floor with a grating round it. After the first day these over-flowed and were shut up and henceforth we had to go across the barrack square to the open air lavatories. Day or night one had to make this trip across the snow and use these filthy holes cleaning ones shoes afterwards as well as one could in the snow. It was the worst trial of all.

By now there were four or five thousand people in the three big buildings, among them 500 nuns – There appeared to be no drainage system at all – All the slops had to be emptied in open drains in the courtyard, these overflowed and a smelly stream began to surround our building. Fortunately there was a severe frost all this time so everything froze hard. Each drain had several yards of ice round it and emptying pails was quite a dangerous job.

German soldiers came and told us that 35 people must be housed in our room so we put all our beds together in one half of the room and another lot of people came into the other half. By putting our beds very close we hoped to avoid the double decker beds which were being put up in the other rooms. Many people were ill and were taken across to the Infirmary. All of us had coughs and colds and the noises that went on at night made sleep difficult. After ten days of this life Kathleen was so ill she was taken off on a stretcher by two soldiers and after a week there to the hospital in the town. Patients leaving the infirmary often spent several hours out of bed on a stretcher or on their feet waiting about in the snow – their near relations or friends not able to go with or get news of them once they had gone.

I got leave to go to the hospital about once in 3 weeks if I could get a seat in the ambulance, but soon so many were going to see sick relations that we were sent on foot guarded by several soldiers. We were a draggled looking crowd many in blue soldier's coats much too big for them. We had been given these coats and I personally lived in mine and at night they went on the beds. We were very glad to walk and see a little of the town.

The days passed quickly as we were busy, if waiting for hours in the snow can be called busy. At 8 o'c one of us went for the "coffee", at 11 o'c two of us went for the potatoes and perhaps an inch of meat – At 6 o'c we went for the evening meal of "coffee" and a spoonful of lard or jam or cheese. Then we had to queu up for letters, parcels, if lucky enough to get one, and bread. There was a cantine [small army-controlled shop], but it meant waiting in the snow sometimes for an hour or more to get a piece of pain d'épice [a type of sweet bread] or an apple. There was not nearly enough for everybody.

Every drop of water for washing ourselves and our clothes had to be carried up our 50 odd steps and all carried down again in pails and emptied in the outside gratings. Water was often upset on the steps, this froze so that there was a thin coating of ice over them.

'Chambre 61, Bâtiment C.'

Our midday soup was made of potatoes and mangold wurzles; or "nouilles" [pasta] and potatoes, or barley and potatoes, or cabbage. Nourishing but not appetising and everything had a curious taste. The potatoes were mostly bad and often frozen. We had to peel them in a shed, freezing cold and the potatoes hard and crystallized with frost. We each had to go twice or three times a week. Some utterly refused to go but it only made more work for the others. Besides the fearful cold for ones hands the potatoes smelt very bad. One day we struck and refused to touch them the smell was so bad – The French prisoners in charge of the job sent for the German sentinels – these could do nothing with an angry mob of women so they in turn fetched the Kommandant. He unfortunately was in the middle of his lunch so arrived in a furious temper and stormed at us in bad French. He said what was good enough for Germans was good enough for us. We had been parading about with potatoes stuck on knives but we all meekly returned to our benches, we were afraid of going to the lock up. This

'Potato peeling.'

job did not improve our colds but very fortunately we could buy excellent paper handkerchiefs and these served all sorts of purposes as well such as wiping the dinner table and cleaning shoes as we had no rag of any sort or any cloths. We cut up one of the linen bed sacks and each had a small piece as a towel. I had brought a towel and a very useful apron with me.

We nearly all had chronic colds besides colics and indigestion – Sleep was difficult, the room was never quiet so many people coughing or snoring and beds creaking. Lights out at 9.30 when a bugle call went.

1941 Jan. 8th Workmen are making indoor lavatories, we feel it means we are in here for some time if they are for us. We were given paper to write on Dec 12th and again on the 29th but we have reason to doubt if these letters were ever sent. (Ours did not arrive) (On the journey we had dropped notes out of the window wrapped up with five francs. Some of these reached home.) I have had several letters and two parcels from home but no mention of my letters. We wrote again 2 days ago on forms given us – only a few sentences and very clearly.

We are now supplementing our food with oranges, apples and pain d'épice from the cantine and anything sent from home in parcels or brought into the caserne [barracks] by workmen – These men are always ready to help us and run a great risk by so doing. They lately got us some ham which was a real pleasure. One can also buy beer or lemonade at the cantine but it means a wait of an hour or so in the cold.

We live in a constant state of dirt. We have one small very worn out broom for the whole room. We have so far had 1½ cubic inches of soap for washing ourselves and our clothes. None can be spared for the washing up and the water is very hard. We wash up in the same basin as we

'Chambre 61.'

wash ourselves in. We had the cement floor washed once by a Polish woman. It took her all day. Each of the 24 beds had to be moved in turn, the baggage stacked up and many buckets of water fetched and emptied.

What we principally want is soap and overalls or aprons. We have no sheets or pillows but could not wash or dry them if we had. Most of us have French army blue overcoats – 'la capotte', breeches and a few of us enormous wooden soled boots.

Jan. 10th A parcel came from Ciboure for me! A pillow, half a big piece of soap which was received with shouts by the whole room, also 4 towels. The latter very welcome after using one small one for 5 weeks. No one has enough soap to wash anything properly. We are warm in the room

'View from my bed.'

'Bread day.'

with a stove each end. Ours burns well but the other half of the room has trouble with theirs. We sometimes cant see across the room for the thick black smoke.

Having had 3 falls on the very slippery ice covered ground I am feeling rather sore. A nice little masseuse has been rubbing my back twice a day. Rather a public performance. She has also given beauty treatment to one or two faces in the room. She takes no payment.

Workmen are still hard at work on the new lavatories. Two sets of 8 on each floor with seats and flush of water. None are finished yet, nor the drains. We are all wondering for whom are they being built. If for us it means a long stay I'm afraid. The wind is bitter today but all the same about 100 people are waiting outside the cantine. They have already waited an hour.

Jan. 11th Had a wonderful night on my new pillow, breakfast in bed of white bread, brought in from town by a workman, butter and tea. Stove lit for us by 2 old men, former stable lads who have also taken down the pails. We have an arrangement now for this job, they also fetch our coal and wood.

One of our party was taken shopping by the German nurse. We gave her many commissions but she found nothing to buy but a few onions which we cooked with lentils given us by some nuns. The shop people were very agreeable and sympathetic all seemed sorry for us.

I spent 2 hours in a room occupied by nuns, 25 of them mostly in double-decker beds. They were so pleased with my sketches, I have left them busily copying them so as to send them home eventually. The nuns perched up on the top beds with legs dangling down looked quite comic. I think a good many of the younger ones are quite pleased with the adventure. Their convents send them lots of parcels and they eat better than we do.

Jan. 12th, Sunday Another call by French soldiers for potato peelers. I went 2 days ago. One stood or sat if you could find a bench, in a shed with the floor covered with potatoes, frozen and in different stages of decay. The hardest are picked out and peeled, or rather the skin is chipped off like bits of ice. They are covered with wet and frozen icey mud and it is difficult to see what is peeled and what is not. Hands get frozen and black with mud above the wrists. Small stoves are now put in the shed but as they have no chimneys the air becomes a bit thick with smoke. Tempers also get short. As soon as the pile gets a bit low more potatoes are shot through the window followed by enormous mangold wurzels. These latter quite frozen also and needing great strength to get the skin off after being split in half by a soldier with a hatchet. I left after one and a half hours but was angrily followed by the soldier in charge who threatened to send a German after me. I told him he could do just what he liked, that I had done 1½ hours and had had enough. This I shouted over my shoulder as we were both running. I hope when I go next that he wont remember me. The potatoes once peeled and cut up are thrown into boxes, taken away and put in big iron tubs where they remain frozen until cooked for our meals. They remain hard when cooked and almost uneatable. They are our principal food, its no wonder so many of us are ill.

'Tea time.'

Just been served with one small tablet of soap for 10 of us. This is the 2nd distribution in 5 weeks, the first was a tiny bit of yellow soap each, mostly composed of pumice stone.

After I had left the potato shed without leave I heard that the Frenchman made remarks about the English which were not well received by the peelers, all very British. They pelted him with bad potatoes until he was obliged to escape and fetch German soldiers to protect him and restore order. The Germans were quite good humoured over it.

Jan 13th Only a small proportion of the interned are really British. Many French women with English husbands. Most of the stable lads and jockeys have French wives. Also any person who happened to be born in a British possession. I tried to go down to the hospital to see Kathleen, fifteen people went on foot in charge of a German soldier but I could not get permission. I may go next Friday.

There is a committee of English women formed and another of men. They have organised the distribution of letters and parcels. Lists are put up for parcels, out of doors. To reach them you cross 2 metres of frozen slop water coming from the kitchen. If your name is on the list you wait in a queue for your parcel. The parcel is opened before you by a German, examined and any books or written matter kept to go before the censor.

The committee has also formed a squad of police women to stand all day outside the cold water washing rooms. To prevent slops or refuse being thrown into the troughs and floor drains. Many persons threw slops etc here and the drains or gratings in the floor all got stopped up. Also an old man cleans up the lavatories as well as he can – Today the big tins underneath are full to the brims but it is not his job to empty them – soldiers come with carts – The old man whose name is Bottom often rescues watches money etc. which fall from pockets.

Except for 2 or 3 days thaw we have quite deep snow all the time. It gets trodden down into slippery paths of frozen snow. Many crows visit

'Sawing up a stolen plank when fuel was getting scarce.'

'A small room for six nuns.'

the yard as there is a good deal of food round the different drains. So often the midday meal is uneatable and much gets thrown away.

Jan 14th Excitement last night as our 2nd bug was caught. The first about 10 days ago visited me – but got away after biting my face, neck and wrists. They live many of them behind the black iron boxes above each bed. The room being very warm they are enticed out. Vauban colic also enlivened the night. For dinner today we had a soup of rice and barley

'Nuns in small room.'

and a few scraps of meat, but I did not get any meat – The nuns had again given us lentils so we had a good meal.

Yesterday many people were taken ill in Batiment A – we are Batiment C, in the night. Doctors were there all night. We are getting nervous about our health, we never get rid of our colds and coughs and frequent attacks of dysentery. The kitchen is at fault – so dirty and rats playing about among the potatoes.

Our room is really warm, it's the saving of us, though it does bring out the bugs. They walk on the ceiling and as soon as the lights are out they drop on the beds. Some of us get devoured every night. Last night there was no water and none today – We collect the snow and melt it.

Friday Went to the hospital with 20 others in charge of two German soldiers. I wore my blue soldiers coat. Enjoyed seeing a bit of the town which is very picturesque. The hospital is a very interesting old building with courtyards and cloisters and immense wards with 60 and 80 patients in each.

Received 2 very welcome parcels from home, especially the butter.

Jan 18th More snow fallen but warmer. Went to town to dentist with German nurse. Coming back stopped at bookshop to buy a latin grammar for Kathleen. The shop girl slipped into the parcel a map of Europe which I wanted, without the nurse noticing. This map was always much in request afterwards and went the round of the rooms.

Had half the ammount of soup today – food getting scarce I suppose. Potatoes and nouilles [pasta] in the soup and scrap of leather-like meat quite uneatable but it gives a flavour. Had cheese and dates from private store. Spend my time drawing the people in the room, have had some coloured pencils sent from home.

Sunday Sauerkraut and potatoes for dinner and hard biscuits and spoonful of jam for supper. Snow melting, very slippery and smelly as the heaps of rubbish everywhere begin to thaw.

Went to the potato peeling today but it was much better than usual. The potatoes were not frozen, the shed warmer and less potatoes. We finished in one hour and felt so gay we all sang lustily while at work. French songs led by one of the men cooks.

Jan 20th Snow melting fast. Have been drawing all day. Have only very poor paper.

Jan 21st Had 2 letters and 2 parcels. They had only now received my first letter. Cheese only for supper. Many rumours about our going away from here.

22nd Caught another bug in the night, am all over bites. Snow all gone, much mud.

23rd All received Red Cross parcels! wonderful parcels with sweets, soap, dates, chocolate, tea, sugar, margarine and different tins of vegetables, fish and meat. No more sweet tisane in the morning but a good cup of tea made over the stove. A spoonful of grease for

supper – I put it on my shoes. Weather warmer our stoves quite oppressive and bugs very lively.

24th Two from our room left. The husband of one had died but she was not told of it till 15 days after. We are quieter and more comfortable. Mud and water round our building getting worse. We have to go over planks to get in at the doors. Grease again for supper.

Feb 2nd Snow again. Things are now much better here as the W.Cs are in use, not all working well but it makes an immense difference not having to go out of doors. Also today the potatoes were neither frozen or rotten and 1½ hrs under the better conditions is bearable. The mangold wurzles are more tiring. 4 letters from home.
Feb 3rd W.Cs stopped up for want of water – we go out of doors again. Supper a small spoonful of jam.

Feb 4th Every thing frozen hard again. Have not been out, too slippery. Had a pudding of dates and pain d'épice made over our stove. Very good indeed. The other people in the room mostly sit about and read or play patience or go for walks round and round the barrack square. Of course washing up and washing clothes, fetching meals and water, emptying pails etc gives us something to do. I am fortunate in having an occupation that I like. When sunny enough I go to the stables and draw the big horses there, otherwise I have no lack of models in the room. Some weeks ago we were all given a bed cover of blue checked cotton, and from an extra one we made a curtain, hung it between the windows with a small table behind it. This makes a good washing place for us. Each side of the room has this arrangement.

We have all been moved out of our room for it to be disinfected. Seven of us are in a small room, so small we have to eat on our beds – Our big room is sealed up. Each room is being done in turn. Batiment A has already been done and the bugs are worse than ever.

Some people tell me that Kathleen has left for home but others say she is still there. We may not go to the hospital as some women managed to escape on the way there – Not the first to escape by any means, in spite of the double row of barbed wire with a broad barbed wire entanglement in between the 2 rows. Sentinels all round outside and at night they walk round and round the buildings.

Feb. 18th Influx of eight more people into our room – while their room is being de-bugged. Double deck beds and some sleeping on the tables. No more peace for us. One has brought a dog.

Feb. 27th Believe Kathleen has really left for home. Warm, sat out in the sun. Our room much more pleasant as we are less thick on the ground.

April 27th Our chef du Batiment [the prisoner chosen to supervise the barrack block] has returned after 2 months in prison making paper bags. She disappeared one day and later Germans took away a few toilette articles but no one knew why or where she had gone. She accompanied a friend whose husband had died of pneumonia at the hospital to the funeral. She was indignant at the way it was done and said before others that he had "been buried like a dog". This had no doubt been reported.

We have been told to pack all our goods ready for disinfecting all except food (our Red Cross parcels) and toilette things for some days and for journey. We now know we are going to Vittel. At 11 o'c when lights were out the police came and told us to be ready with our baggage to go to the Infirmary at 2 a.m! None of us moved, but other rooms got up and dressed.

April 28th Ordered to the Infirmary after lunch. Our heavy baggage taken by soldiers. We opened the trunks and left them piled up in a small room. At 3 o'c we went back to shut them when with great difficulty we had found them & again left them. The bugs were supposed to have been killed by fumes and heat. Our batiment was finished some time in the night. We had all kept out a good many things which we were afraid might be spoilt by the process.

My drawings had little by little left the barracks and reached home – but this was not done openly as it was forbidden.

In the evening we were told that Batiment A was to go to the douches [showers] at 6 o'c in the morning, their clothes would be taken and blankets given, to walk thus clad to the Infirmary and there wait while the clothes were fumigated. Bat. A objected, about 600 of them and asked us to come and demonstrate at 5.30 next morning, but to be silent and well behaved.

After a bad night we all got up and went out on the square in the dark. German officers and soldiers were there, the heads of the English committees spoke to them and then ordered everybody except Bat. A back to their rooms and that then Bat A could speak. We retired very slowly but before we reached our doors the Germans fired 3 shots. Women screamed, some fled but most stood their ground. We waited our end of the yard, some 20 nuns with us. Bat. A was forced indoors by soldiers we also and told not to come out or appear at the windows. Of course we went at once to the windows and saw 50 soldiers arrive at a trot to the middle of the square, there they stacked their guns. Presently 2 by 2 the women came from Bat. A each with a towel and paper and string for their clothes. The douches are very primitive, the floors very dirty, no where to put your clothes and you go in two together. Only a trickle of water. I went once but it was quite enough. There are 500 people in A and only 10 douches working. They are supposed to take the train this evening and have received dry biscuits and ½ loaf each. We are all feeling very jumpy and several in the room are not well.

April 30th We got up early and went down to the douches. Nobody I think went under the douches or took off more than their coats and dresses which were piled on hand carts and taken away. We waited for our clothes in a building near the douche. Once clothed again we sat about on our valises and hand baggage till about 11 o'c when we started for the station.

We did not go to the station near by but had a walk of one hour. We were very heavily laden and looked like Polish refugees with pots and pans and bags, baskets and suit cases. Every few minutes the whole procession stopped to rest. Two French women joined us and helped carry some baggage, but as we did not go through the town we did not see many people. When we came to a field full of spring flowers the whole procession stopped to exclame and admire and our guards had difficulty

'Waiting to start for Vittel' – a self-portrait.

to make us move on. At last we reached the train and were put six in each carriage and in ours a fully armed soldier. A rolling kitchen came along about 10 o'c with hot soup.

We spent the rest of the day and all the next night in the train, arriving in Vittel in the morning. We very much enjoyed the scenery, the green fields and trees especially, after five months of the barrack square. But the nearer we got to Vittel the less interesting it became. Our spirits began to go down. The night had been very very cold. We had enlivened the journey by writing letters, hands and paper hidden behind the lid of a suitcase so that the German should not see. We folded them up small with a five franc note and then waited to throw them out to a likely looking workman on the line or an official. This could not be done in the stations. One had to wait till the train was going slowly, no Germans about and catch the eye of a likely looking man near the train. Also our guard had to be occupied by one of us talking broken German to him. It was very difficult to get all the necessary conditions at the same moment. Two out of my three letters reached their port.

VITTEL

At Vittel station we loaded up again with our traps and started for the hotel. A funny looking procession none the better for our night in the train, all ages, all sorts, fur coats, military coats, pots pans and traps of all shapes and sizes. We had had no breakfast and the spirits of myself and friends was very low. The country looked deadly, so did the small town and the many shut up hotels. A most depressing class of place at the best of times.

We came to the big hotel we were to inhabit. Batiments A and B were already installed. The hotel a whited sepulchre was surrounded with the inevitable barbed wire of course, it had been shut up for 2 years, there was no heating and it was extremely cold with frosts at night. We found the room allocated to us four and with difficulty evicted a coloured woman and another. Our beds almost touched as the room was small. It had a bathroom with W.C. but no window and no water as the pipes had burst. One electric light in the middle of the room. It is called a first class hotel but we were not in the more modern part. The beds were good with sommiers [proper bases], such a change for us also we were given sheets and pillow cases. The beds felt damp and cold but there was no means of getting hot water for bottles or even a cup of tea. We were rather depressed and I for one was already thinking that dirt and warmth were preferable to cold and cleanliness. Painting seemed impossible in such a place and how were we going to live without our tea!

These first weeks have been very uncomfortable owing to the lack of hot water and the cold. Although it is May there are still frosts and the trees are as bare as in the depth of winter.

In the morning we go down to a big dining room set with trestles and chairs and have black sweet tisane – very nasty. We take bread and margarine with us. Dinner begins at 11 o'c. We queue up for it in the same room. Potatoes and nouilles [pasta], or orge [barley], sometimes a hard scrap of meat with a spoonful of quite good gravy. But a clean kitchen makes a lot of difference the potatoes etc. taste good.

We get our excellent Red Cross parcels every week, an unfailing pleasure. From these we have a nice dessert of dates or chocolate or jam in our room.

Most of us manage to send some of these good things home. There are always workmen from outside doing jobs in the hotel or in the grounds. There are some in the kitchen and others are putting in central heating in the 700 bedrooms. These men are ready to risk imprisonment and fines by taking our parcels and sending them off in their own name. They are often searched and some get caught. We give them cigarettes or a tin of dripping.

'The Vittel swan.'

As the central heating will not be ready in time they are putting stoves in all the rooms. These stoves are put on squares of concrete and the pipes taken out through the windows. Black smoke pours out of many rooms and also the smoke from our neighbours comes in at the windows. We shall soon be as black as in Vauban. There is a real danger from fire too and no fire drill or precautions taken.

In June we had some nice days and could enjoy the Park. The trees were very fine, there was a small pond with a swan on it and 1000s of rats on an island in the middle. We were not allowed on the grass except in the childrens playing field. Several squirells gave us great pleasure but they never became very tame – too many people to scream and point at them. The birds also are interesting. Nuthatches and redstarts have nests every where, there are also tits and green-woodpeckers.

In June a cuisine roulante [mobile camp kitchen] which supplied the morning tisane was allowed to boil up water in the afternoon for tea. It was beseiged every day soon after lunch by people waiting for the water to boil which was any time after 3 o'c. A long queu formed with different sorts of pots, tins or cups. A few lucky ones had tea pots, many only condensed milk tins held by a bit of string. There was never enough water for every body. After six weeks another rolling kitchen was given us. This was in charge of an English woman who enrolled 50 helpers and then we had hot water for tea or bottles all day. She was the most popular woman in camp. It was hard work and she got up at 4.30 every morning to light the fires. We could then have tea for our breakfasts.

At the end of September it was too cold out of doors so she was given an unused kitchen below the annex of the hotel. Water here was boiled up in 3 enormous washing cauldrons, a fire under each. Also the big ovens were started and everyone could heat up their tins of pork and beans etc. and make cakes from breadcrumbs and egg powder, all from our parcels. Wonderful dishes were evolved.

One day the head of our kitchen was called to the Kommandature, she did not come back and we found that she was in the lock-up. We managed to speak to her at the window before the sentinel drove us away. The camp was very indignant.

She was also in charge of a small dining room and had taken off the 60 covers of the tables to have them washed. For the night they were put in a cupboard. Next day there were only 20 covers. We were all so short of underclothes and cloths that anything left about was quickly pinched.

'Tea time at Vittel.'

'Early morning tea urns.'

It was given out that M^rs G would remain in prison until the covers were returned. By next day all but 10 or so were back, some already cut up into garments. M^rs G was released from the lock-up which was in the Park itself. For more serious crimes there was another prison.

Games were in full swing in the summer, tennis, until the rackets gave out which was very soon, deck tennis basket ball, folk dancing, gymnastics ping pong and bowls. Then in October a sad end came to the games – The head of the "Games" got into trouble with the authorities and "disappeared" I think to a camp in Germany. No one would take her place out of a feeling of loyalty, so all came to a full stop. It was a great pity, many girls had nothing to do and the morale of the camp was rapidly getting worse.

In December the central heating was working in one part of the hotel. It did not heat much and big coats were necessary in the rooms. It was exceptionally cold. The park looked very pretty under snow. Hot water in the bathrooms was very erratic, we would be weeks without any in our part of the building and then get it for a few hours only. The water

'The Grand Hotel dining room.'

was extremely hard, quite impossible to get a lather with any soap. As we had to wash our plates and dishes in our basins they soon got stopped up with grease etc.

We were supplied with one meal a day – our tea and supper were made from our Red + parcels and eaten in our rooms.

In the Park was a covered arcade with shops on one side, but all shut up and empty of course. Some were taken for storing bread and one for the cantine. One could sometimes get fruit at the cantine or vegetables, cheese and always paper handkerchiefs. There was also a shop for luxurious stuffs, handbags and jewellery. The prices were enormous but some people still had money. A coiffeur came from Vittel and did a big business. It was strange how many women had dyed hair. Before leaving Besançon the piebald heads were very numerous. In Vittel they recovered their reds and auburns and waviness. During the summer the Casino in the grounds began to function every week but the films shown were very poor. Every 2 months or so the internees gave a very good show – Acting and dancing and singing. There was quite a lot of talent among

'Rue Baignol, Ciboure.'

them. There were also lectures on various subjects and classes for learning English, French, Spanish, German and Russian. A good many people painted and worked seriously with what materials they could get. When I left in Dec. we had already a good library.

In fine weather one walked or sat about in the Park. We could drink the waters, feed the swan and watch the antics of the rats. It took eleven minutes to make the tour of the Park. The catholic church was in the park and an Irish priest officiated. The protestants had a service in the Casino.

Dec 6th 1941 In Dec I left [because she was 60]. I was given 200 fs and my ticket to Ciboure 3rd class. I had to spend the night in Dijon as there was no train till next day and had difficulty in finding a room or getting anything to eat as of course I had no food cards. The train near Tours was held up some hours because of an "alerte", finally I arrived at 3 o'c in the afternoon, one day and five hours late but overjoyed at being at last free. It was rather a surprise to find a barbed wire entanglement outside our own gate and a sentinel walking up and down day and night. But the house opposite and one alongside were both occupied by Germans and our road is one of the roads to Spain.

1. Aunt Fan posing with her brand new Peugeot, in 1938.

2. Aunt Fan's Father, Major-General Edward D'Oyley Twemlow.

3. Aunt Fan's Mother, Margret Twemlow.

Right: 4. Kathleen, Hubert and Fan, in about 1888.

Below: 5. Family group about 1900 (left to right): Edward Twemlow, Dora, 'Mab' Twemlow, Fan.

Above: 6. Molly, Fan, two friends and Kathleen, in France in the 1930s.

Below: 7. Aunt Fan (right) on a painting expedition with a friend.

8. The House at Ciboure.

9. Ciboure.

Right: 10. Aunt Fan's cottage.

Below: 11. Mules.

Above: 12. Near the gatehouse of Caserne Vauban, Besançon.

Below: 13. 'Debugging' (coloured illustration from the diary).

F Twemlow   9am 4ª
1941

14. Besançon parade ground in snow.

Above: 15. Stella Gumuchian's sketch, 'Firewood Under a Bed.'

Below: 16. 'Boots and breeches.'

Right: 17. 'Hilda.'

Below: 18. 'Conversation Piece.'

19. 'The Grand Hotel, Vittel' (coloured illustration from the diary).

20. 'The Vittel Park' (coloured illustration from the diary).

Vittel
1921

21. Mrs Cashman playing the cello.

22. Mat from Besançon, embroidered with the signatures of those who shared Aunt Fan's room.

Left: 23. The diary cover.

Below: 24. St Jean-de-Luz harbour.

5

Filth, Food and Frosts: Besançon 1940-1941

From the German point of view, Besançon was, in many respects, a convenient place to intern civilians. It was relatively close to the German border, in the more heavily militarised zone; it had good rail links; and it had four substantial military establishments, distributed around the deeply incised meander of the River Doubs which enclosed the city. There were three forts, part of the defences designed by the great seventeenth-century military engineer Vauban. The most prominent of these was the Citadel high up on the central hill, with two smaller but equally strategic forts on the hilltops on either side. Lastly, there was an army barracks on the low ground at the far side of the city, to the north-west; it was here, Caserne Vauban, that the camp called Frontstalag 142 was established.

As soon as the armistice with the French Government was signed in 1940, the German army of occupation began to plan a systematic arrest and detention of men between the ages of sixteen and sixty-five who were in possession of British papers. About a thousand such men and boys were known to have remained in northern France rather than escaping to England, and they were rounded up and held at several separate camps, notably the St Denis barracks near Paris. Then, in November 1940, the decision was made to extend this internment to all British citizens except adolescents, regardless of age or sex, and to most citizens of the British Commonwealth and Empire. For some time previously, it had been necessary to register regularly with the local authorities, and so this round-up was easily organised. Women, young children, and a few elderly men were gathered together and packed into trains, and sent off to an unknown destination. A small advance party may have reached Besançon on or soon after 2 December, but the great majority arrived, as Aunt Fan did, about six days later. In January 1941, the German authorities used information from the French police to compile a list of about 400 more British civilians whom they believed were still living in France. About half of these were located, arrested and brought to Besançon towards the end of February.

The people of Besançon seem to have had no warning of the arrival of the internees, and their transfer from the trains to the barracks was kept as secret as possible. The barracks had previously been used for some of the thousands of French (and a few British) military prisoners of war, who had mostly by now been moved to Germany or put to work in the occupied zone. One of these prisoners was Lieutenant Gillet, a French army doctor who had been held at a camp north of Besançon before being transferred to Caserne Vauban at the end of November. Colonel Dutriez, a member of the Besançon Academy, interviewed Dr Gillet after the war and recorded his experiences for a local journal. On his arrival at the Caserne, Gillet had found the Germans in the process of deporting thousands of prisoners of war to Germany, but he and his four medical colleagues, three French and one Polish, were told they were to be kept behind. They soon noticed a working party beginning to construct some sort of a sewerage system, and attempts being made to clean and 'disinfect' the barrack blocks. A few days later, these doctors were astonished to be awoken at one o'clock in the morning and ordered to a reception area by the barrack gates. To their amazement, they saw the first of the internees, whom they at once recognised as English, arriving from the railway station in a piteous condition. It was Dr Gillet and his four fellow medics, then, who helped to transfer the five hundred most elderly and sick internees, together with the mothers with tiny children, straight to the civilian hospital in the city.

The barracks were arranged around a central square, half of which was the old parade ground and the remainder was a sports circuit. The three main accommodation blocks, two on one side and one on the other, were each four stories high, and known simply as Bâtiments A, B and C respectively. They had stone floors, small high windows, and worn stone central staircases. Each level was subdivided into big rooms, many now bare of furniture. At the parade ground end of the barracks, near the gate onto the highway, was an infirmary, the Kommandant's lodgings and office, a small shack containing 'long drop' privies, and a non-functioning shower block, together with a central war memorial facing onto the parade ground. Behind Bâtiment C, on the city side of the barracks, was a long, single-storey building which contained the offices from which bread and parcels would later be handed out, the kitchen and the cellar where potato-peeling duties would take place, and at the far end a chapel. Behind the sports circuit, there were other privies, a stable block, stores for wood, coal and straw, a lock-up, and some additional small accommodation blocks including one for the French soldiers who had been retained at the barracks to help with guard duties.

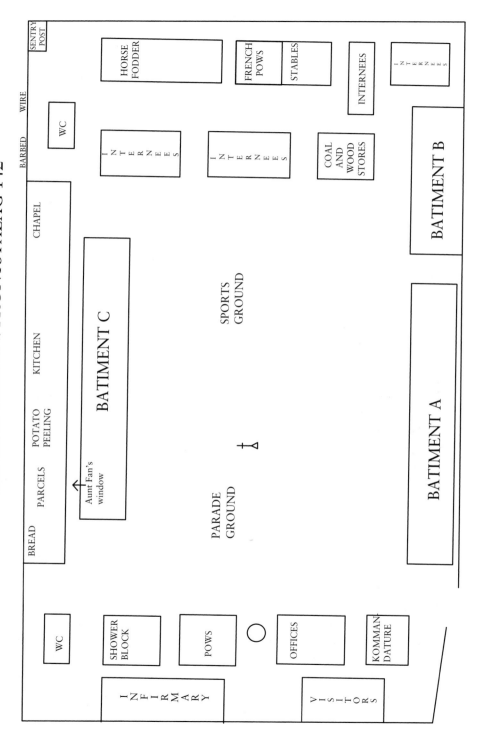

CASERNE VAUBAN: FRONTSTALAG 142

SENTRY POST

BARBED WIRE

HORSE FODDER

FRENCH POWS

STABLES

INTERNEES

INTERNEES

WC

INTERNEES

INTERNEES

COAL AND WOOD STORES

BATIMENT B

CHAPEL

BATIMENT C

KITCHEN

SPORTS GROUND

POTATO PEELING

PARCELS

Aunt Fan's window

BREAD

PARADE GROUND

BATIMENT A

WC

SHOWER BLOCK

POWS

OFFICES

KOMMANDATURE

INFIRMARY

VISITORS

Not much of this detail, however, was apparent to the internees when they first arrived. There had been so many French prisoners, squeezed into the barrack blocks and in tents in the central square, that the mess left behind could not have been cleaned up properly, even if the Germans had wanted to. The square was covered with heaps of rubbish and filthy, discarded army equipment, mixed in with the mounds of snow and frozen slush. Inside the barracks, most of the floors were covered with icy water, left over from the attempt to swill them out.

Fernande Oldfield, the young couturier who had been born in London, was sent to Bâtiment B where she was convinced that the mess had been left deliberately:

> The French prisoners of war who had prepared the rooms, believing that it would be German women coming in, had thrown buckets of water all over the floor. The straw mattresses which should have been our beds were missing, and seeing their mistake the French POWs lit great stoves and made a blazing inferno. But despite this damp heat we shivered and were unable to sleep. It should also be said that we had not eaten nor drunk for nearly two days.
>
> The barracks had been stripped bare. Our room was so dirty and disgusting, the walls were more black than grey, and Oh the smell!

Mabel Bayliss had a similar first impression:

> … the barrack gate opened and we crossed a filthy, muddy court-yard and were told to go into the building. The ground floor was very dark, so my friend and I rushed up to the first floor; seeing huge empty rooms, wet everywhere, we quickly ventured to the second floor. There, it was just the same. Later on we learnt that twenty thousand prisoners of war had recently left the barracks and had been ordered to throw pails of water down to clean the stone floors. The straw mattresses were literally floating. My friend found an old garden broom and swept the water away. We chose two mattresses and stood them up against the dirty wall to dry. All of us were feeling tired, hungry, and longing for a cup of tea. Alas! there was nothing.

Frida Stewart and Rosemary Say, who were in their late twenties and escaped together from the camp at Vittel in 1942, wrote an account of their time in internment shortly after their arrival home in England. They too were appalled by their first sight of the barracks:

> An escort of Nazi troops marched us into the courtyard of the Besançon barracks on December 6th, 1940. Our first impression of Cazerne Vauban,

three huge blocks with outhouses and offices built round a cinder court, and surrounded by high walls festooned with barbed wire, was peculiarly depressing. Two days before our arrival, some twenty thousand French and English prisoners of war, taken there from the Maginot line the previous June, had been transferred to Germany from the barracks. They had left behind them an indescribable chaos; the place was littered with old military coats, helmets, rusty tins and utensils of all sorts, and the floors and stairs were swimming in mud, all this in spite of heroic efforts to clean up the Augean stables by the hundred French soldiers who remained.

These were specialised workmen, kept on by the Germans to serve in the camp as plumbers, carpenters, cobblers and mechanics, and in the offices and stables, under German orders. When demobilised later, they were replaced by Senegalese. German officers directed the administration and we were guarded of course, by German sentries in full battle dress.

Patricia McGauley, the young English nun who had been arrested in Angers, found herself in the basement of Bâtiment C, the same block as Aunt Fan, but after their circuitous journey she and her fellow Sisters arrived two days later, when many of the rooms were already full:

It was snowing when we arrived and our lot was sent to Bâtiment C. We were told to look for rooms and to fetch our baggage afterwards. The sight of Bâtiment C our future home was a nightmare to us! God help us, the worst had not yet been seen! We went inside! It would be impossible to describe our first impressions! We went into a hall thronged with people. I had visions of the market hall in Birmingham. But it was much worse and oh so dirty! We toiled up the stairs in the crush in search for rooms and what rooms we saw! Very long with pieces of wood jutting out of the wall at intervals as in stables. In each 'stall' was a wooden bed and a good many were double deckers! These rooms were full of women and screaming children and dogs etc.

I can still hear Sister Mary of St Cecilia asking us if it was hell! We were dead tired and after traipsing up and down the stairs of four storeys Sister Mary of St Teresa who spoke fluent German went in search of an officer to find a room for us. By this time the Nazareth Sisters had gone their separate way.

Finally we were given a room on the ground floor – seeing how small it was I felt I had to suggest that we too should also find our own accommodation – but the six Good Shepherd sisters from Angers wouldn't hear of it. We were given no. 19 and it was actually a coal cellar. Whilst it was being cleared we crossed a lane behind Bâtiment C and went into a hall (the chapel). There we found 200 Little Sisters Of The Poor. They kindly offered us some of their potatoes and gave us a hot drink.

No 19 in Bâtiment C ... was 12' x 6' and it was to be our home for the next six months. Somebody brought along a big red bowl of pea soup – no dishes – just spoons! We all dipped in, too tired to care! Later on eight straw mattresses were flung in. We placed them side by side in a row from window to door. So we slept in one large bed! In those days we all wore night caps, and a good thing too! When we got up in the morning we had all been crowned with a black patch where our heads had touched the walls. It was so funny!

The following morning four double decker beds were fixed for us, two on each side, which left just enough space between the beds and the door for a small stove. The only other space in the room was the narrow passage between the beds. So we were given two trestles and a plank which served as a table. We had two narrow benches for six of us, and the remaining two had to sit on a bucket at each end of the table. There we ate, slept and washed when we could get water. When possible we collected a bowl of water at night and all eight of us washed in it the following morning. Otherwise we just went outside and rubbed our faces in the snow.

Our door had no key but when we slammed it to, it locked itself. The only way of opening it was with our pen knives. Fortunately I had told my mother that the mother-of-pearl pen knife that she had bought for me wasn't suitable, it had to be a boy scout's knife. It was the only one which didn't break when being used as a key. And lucky we were to have it! It was quite frightening sometimes at night when drunken soldiers came hammering on our door.

We took it in turns to light the fire in the mornings. One day in desperation Sister Mary Catherine couldn't get it alight so she turned to the Benedictine nuns from Bayeux, next door, for help. They told her to follow their example and take some straw from her mattress.

Samuel Hales, the elderly New Zealander, was put in room 76 of Bâtiment C. He wrote an account of his time at Besançon in 1946, while it was fresh in his memory:

I slept for the first eight days on the bare floor. Fortunately, I had a heavy winter coat to cover me, otherwise I should have frozen to death, as it was the beginning of one of the worst winters for 50 years. It seemed to be snowing perpetually and as we had no heating for the first month, a great many died, unable to stand the cold and the bad nourishment ...

After eight days I managed to get a bed and mattress with one blanket. This seemed like a luxury. In the second month we were given a stove and had a certain amount of warmth, one could not say comfort, in a room with 32 men packed in as close as could be. The sanitary arrangements were appalling. We had to cross a courtyard about 50 yards from our rooms, and many died from the cold through having to go out at night with the snow about 6 inches deep, sometimes 12.

We all lost flesh. Although I lost 30 pounds I never gave up hope, and perhaps that kept me alive, as during the three and a half months we were there, about 600 died! They died in such numbers that even the Germans became anxious and allowed all men of 75 years and women over 60 to be liberated. My wife was on the 'free list' but she refused to leave without me. Later I was medically examined by a young doctor and ... I was allowed to go back to Paris.

His wife Elizabeth was in room 86 of Bâtiment A, on the opposite side of the parade ground. She kept her diary going during their time in the camp, and noted the wide variety of people who had been arrested, many of whom were Jews:

with [Sam are] Father George [a monk] and other elderly men also a group of young foreigners – Dutch, Norwegian, Belgian. There is one oldish man, a Jew who suffers from gouty feet and who repeats constantly that he is a rich man. Yet he cannot get away from the camp ... Another man comes from Frankfurt on Mein. Speaks only German and seems one but must be a Jew we think. There is an American who had for some stupid reason taken out a British passport – 68 years old, is in a dreadful state of nerves. One fears he may go out of his mind. Mutters constantly about lack of food and hateful life. A terrible state of affairs. His wife is in hospital – heart trouble. After a time he goes there too and gets out later on reasons of health. His name is Leach.

One day Mrs Hales heard a story from a chance meeting, which perfectly summed up the unnecessary suffering inflicted on these civilian internees:

Meet an old lady on stairs one day – well dressed in fur coat. Tells me she and her daughter came from Paris together. The old, military style – travelled in India etc. Got separated on the journey from her daughter. At a station the girl got down to look for mother. Train began to move. G. soldiers pushed daughter into cattle van at back, took her money off her, kicked her on back, pushed her out at next station, called her *schwein* [pig]. Mistake: she was wearing her brother's military badge, of the English Guards. At Besancon station she fainted and was put in to hospital – back badly injured. Sad story.

In the years since the Second World War, there has been a proliferation of accounts of the brutal treatment of prisoners. Civilians in the Far East, military prisoners of war, forced labour, the indescribable extermination camps and of course much further back the shameful camps of the Boer War, to name but a few. Compassion fatigue is dangerously easy. Yet when Germany initiated World War Two, she was already a signatory to the Third Geneva Convention of 1929, and bound by its regulations. Soon after the War, this was expanded to include more specific and much greater protection for civilians, but the 1929 Convention clearly set out the basic minimum. It agreed that even for military prisoners, treatment was to be humane, and food and accommodation must be of the same standard as that supplied for a combatant nation's own troops. No prisoner should be forced to work, and any work done must be paid employment. Due attention should be paid to the rank and sex of prisoners. Medical facilities, intellectual diversions and sports facilities must be available for prisoners, and 'Adequate clothing should be provided … and sanitary service in camps should be more than sufficient to prevent epidemics.' Last but by no means least, prisoners were to have access to representatives of the International Red Cross, and must be allowed to correspond with their families within the first week of their capture. It is in the context of these international agreements for the treatment of military prisoners of war that the conditions in which the Besançon civilian internees were held should be judged.

The only benefit to be gained from the sordid mess on the barracks square that greeted the prisoners on their arrival was that for many people it provided utensils which were otherwise unavailable at first. The only meal provided on that first day was a sort of soup, one pot per dormitory, and those without spoons or plates were in trouble. Some spoons and communal bowls were given out, but there were not enough to go round; some rooms failed to get any food that day. Many people were reduced to scavenging among the rubbish heaps, as Aunt Fan had to, and scrubbing out any tin or pail they found as best they could with their bare hands, using snow and the grit from the parade ground.

The lack of proper sanitation in the camp was a major problem from the start, although some internees seem to have been aware that conditions were already far worse in the camps in Germany. There was certainly relief that they were being held in France.

There was a single urinal on each floor of the main Bâtiments – small cubicles with a grating in the floor – but few of the hundred or more people per storey managed to use these, and anyway they soon became blocked and were closed off. Temperatures inside these buildings were below zero for much of the time, with icy winds blowing up the stairs. For many weeks the only option was to go out across the square (almost always frosty and covered in snow) to one of the two inadequate sheds containing the privies, variously known by the internees as 'Turkish holes', 'chiottes' or 'tinettes'. These consisted of a large trench, with boards across to make a slatted floor, and holes cut out for seats; there were fewer than twenty privies for an estimated 3,900 people at first. They were supposed to be emptied once a day, and then cleaned out with hot water, but they were generally overflowing and usually frozen, so using them was a horrible ordeal, only ameliorated by the heroic efforts of old 'Mr Bottom', who adopted the wise precaution of calling out 'bottom' in French as he entered. Miss Bayliss was one of the many prisoners who remembered him fondly:

> General hygiene and sanitary arrangements at the barracks were deplorable and the filthy conditions existing were indescribable. Naturally the state of affairs occasioned much hardship, especially among the aged internees. Trenches were made with boards across; a Mr Bottom undertook the cleaning of these places and remarked he had never seen so many bottoms before!
>
> Several months elapsed before sanitary arrangements were improved, even then waiting in a queue was very trying, especially if by chance a priest happened to be there; nuns standing by would reverently exclaim "After you, my Father!"

Elizabeth Hales struggled to find the words to describe the camp latrines:

> The WCs are terrible. And if we are here in summer it will bring epidemic.
>
> I don't like to describe them. Still here goes. The chief one is a wooden building close to batiment A where I live. It is shaped like this. One enters a door and finds a row of wooden planks laid across a deep pit. We are obliged to undress ourselves in front of everyone, and perch ourselves with legs across the hole below.
>
> Rats can be seen from time to time and we know we are not very far from the kit[chen]. It is logic to suppose that they run from wooden house to kitchen – eating up biscuits cheese etc. The thought is awful.
>
> In 3 other parts of the camp there are other WCs, abominably dirty – but more private with closed doors to each one.
>
> To sum things up the worst thing in the camp is the sanitary arrangement.

Mrs Webb, the lady whose son William had been left at home in Senlis, was put in a room up on the top floor of one of the barrack blocks. Here the conditions were if possible even worse than on other floors:

Mother and her little group were shown a fourth floor barrack room by a French Sergeant. He told them the barracks had only just been vacated by 20,000 North African Spahis, Zouaves [French colonial regiments] and Senegalese POWs who were being sent to Germany. There was no heating in the bare barrack rooms, which stank of urine and human faeces littered the concrete floor. Before leaving the POWs were ordered to swill pails of water in an attempt to clean the floors. Soiled, lice ridden, threadbare straw paillasses lay on the concrete, it was the only bedding available and they were damp. Hot water was a rare luxury and could occasionally be obtained from the cook house in a bucket. The toilets, referred to by the POW as the 'chiottes', were in a block outside the building and the filthy conditions prevailing were indescribable. The 'chiottes' consisted of

'Washing arrangements.'

a group of three holes in a row, with half a partition between them and made from rough boards, on which you sat, above the trench. Beneath was a large open pit filled with human waste, the stench was overpowering. The excrement overflowed onto the ground where it froze and was exceedingly slippery and hazardous. The washing bowls, facing the holes, were smashed and the water pipes frozen. There were no other facilities. It was revolting; there was no privacy, no means of keeping themselves or their clothes clean.

Stella Gumuchian, the Armenian brought up in Manchester, had been arrested in Paris together with her sister Sonia and their mother. Unlike Aunt Fan, Stella chose to sketch some of these less pleasant aspects of camp life.

Sketches by Stella Gumuchian.
Above: 'Privies for 4000 people.'
Below: 'French soldiers' old boots.'

As for washing arrangements, there was one communal facility down on the ground floor of each main building. Reminiscent of a cattle trough in a filthy room, these were several metres long, and supplied with cold water through a series of small taps along the sides from overhead pipes. The taps were often covered with icicles, and only the hardiest souls dared to use these rooms. Alternative arrangements were quickly devised by the internees for washing in the dormitories, but even there privacy was severely limited:

At first we had but one tin basin in which to wash and water had to be fetched from the ground floor, many steps below. The majority of us had not even a towel to dry on, neither a rag of any description nor a scrap of paper. Someone tried to arrange a small square cloth on a string behind the door where we could try to wash; no matter at what stage our toilet might be, the Germans entered at any time.

The nuns down in their Room 19 coal cellar worked out a neat solution to the problem of sanitation:

We took it in turns to stay away from Benediction so as to have a good wash down in private. There were no toilets in the buildings – only rooms with a hole in the floor. Awful! Fortunately we had a Foyer Militaire [purser's office] in the camp and they gave out godiots (slang for soldiers boots) and we tied them up with string. One of the worst nightmares was to queue outside that awful toilet when we got up in the morning. Owing to the conditions there was dysentery in the camp and nobody could imagine the rest!

Otherwise we used a bucket in our room at night. We didn't dare go out of our room. That same bucket was part of our seating accommodation during the day. It did have a lid. When we cleaned it we attached it to a piece of string and put it outside our window for an airing! ... The other bucket we filled with water in order to have a reserve for the times the Germans punished us by turning it all off.

On the first morning at Vauban, Aunt Fan's room was awakened by a military bugle:

A Frenchman came in at the bugle call, and told us all to get up. Well, none of us moved; we had each been given one blanket and we were under our blankets and we simply didn't move. So he said 'Oh well, I'll fetch the Germans.' So the Germans came to us, and still nobody moved. I don't know what time it was, but quite early in the morning. But they didn't know what to do, so they left us, fortunately. Later, we fetched a can of black liquid, very sweet and very nasty, too. The food never got better. It was always bad.

Gradually the days fell into a sort of a routine. Each morning began with a bugle call, and then someone from each room went to collect breakfast, which typically consisted of 'coffee' made from mysterious unknown ingredients, together with a small quantity of runny, rancid lard. The main meal, at midday, was a thin and unpleasant soup which occasionally had a few lumps of some sort of meat in it. And for supper there was more 'coffee' and grease, and on good days a little jam or even cheese. Each meal was paid for with tokens, distributed at the start of each week.

The people who collected this food had to stand around in queues in the snow, sometimes for an hour or more, before the rations were handed out. Queuing became a way of life. And then the frozen courtyard and ice-covered steps had to be negotiated to deliver the rations to the rooms. Everyone knew exactly how many steps they had to climb to get back to their room. Each Bâtiment had someone in charge – often someone considered to be 'loyal' by the Germans – and any disaffection was generally reported and punished. For the daily chores, the rooms were left to arrange their own rotas. It soon became apparent that it was not only the German 'sisters' who were spying on the inmates, as private discussions

'Washing up.'

in the rooms often seemed to come to the ears of the authorities. People learnt to be circumspect, and to obey orders as far as possible.

Fernande Oldfield and her friend Hélène, who had been born in British Egypt, were the only two young women in their room, and therefore did most of the fetching and carrying:

> We were put in charge of going to get the wood and coal to feed our stove, which burned day and night. We also brought water, and the midday and evening meals which we carried in huge galvanised buckets. Every time, it was necessary to queue, come rain or snow, for at least an hour, and then climb up our three flights of stairs. It was very heavy going.
>
> The food consisted of rice, pasta, potatoes and swede. At first, we also ate potted meat, but later we only had lard with which to spread our bread. Then came the day when they gave us a white object without any taste, which resembled candle wax, and cheese in tubes, which was all the colours of the rainbow: pink, blue, green. As for the bread, it was soldier's biscuit, made from assorted flours and very dry.

The bread was collected separately, from a store at the back of Bâtiment C, controlled by a French POW. The loaves were always many days old, and very stale; they had the date of baking stamped on top, like a post mark, which was cold comfort for those who had to eat it. Two people from each room had to go for the ration every four days, and when they reached the front of the queue, they handed in their tokens and the bread was thrown out of a window. Most of the time the women managed to catch it in a blanket or cloth held out between them, but too often it all ended up on the ground. But since the loaves were generally green with mould before they were distributed, some extra dirt was not of great note, especially once the internees were organised with rudimentary cutlery, and could remove the worst parts. Many people experimented with toasting their bread against the sides of the grimy stoves, or on improvised pots and pans, but if it was too damp it was inclined to stick, or formed a grim paste. (Later, at Vittel, when there were alternative food sources, this bread was used to make a very useful all-purpose glue).

Sometimes the bread was even more mouldy than normal, and then a protest might be made, but these were seldom successful, as Mabel Bayliss discovered:

> Receiving a specially hard loaf, split like the cliffs of Dover, with the sides absolutely covered with a white-green furry mould, I took it to the Kommandatur. An officer simply produced a large dirty boy-scout kind of knife, bereft the bread of its fur coat, handed it back to me saying, "Now, you can eat it".

One soup a day was given to us, most frequently mangle-wurzel, until we could not even bear the smell of it. Queuing up in a muddy yard for food required patience, especially during the cold snowy weather. The kitchen was filthy and the servers also. Having meat on Sundays, the queue formed many hours before the door opened. We had the satisfaction of frequently waiting by a carcase of a beast, horse I suppose, from which a man hacked off pieces and threw them into a massive iron pot. A few fingers on the man's hands were usually bound up in dirty rags ... Carrying a big metal saucepan of soup for fifteen people in a crowd, across a slippery muddy courtyard, then climbing many stone steps, was not an easy matter; sometimes our hands were too cold to hold the utensil for long, then we took it in turn to stand in the queue.

The field-kitchen from where we fetched our black coffee in the morning was indescribably dirty. We drank it until one day we found a mass of tousled hair at the bottom of the can. Rats were frequent, some seemed as large as rabbits. The awful creatures would tear the sacks of dried vegetables before our very eyes.

Potato and mangel-wurzel peeling duty, and the watery, tasteless and unsavoury stew that was cooked from them, was a perpetual trial. Eventually, a group of women became attached to the kitchen as permanent workers and the peeling was done by 'details' from each Bâtiment in turn. Madeleine Steinberg, née White, who was brought to Besançon with her mother in February 1941 because her father was British, never forgot the odour of cumin that seemed to be the only flavouring which was ever added to the vegetables, and in all her long life she could never bear to have it in her kitchen again.

Madeleine Steinberg at Vittel.

A few of the internees who had been given warning that they were going to be arrested had brought some supplies with them. The La Retraite Sisters had a small stock of tea, that great elixir of English women, which they eked out as long as they could:

> We kept our tea in a cloth tied up with string and just lowered it into the hot water which often didn't boil. We couldn't afford to throw it away but just added a little more tea each time we wanted a cuppa!

At night, everyone suffered from the bed bugs, which became increasingly vicious as time went on. Various ingenious measures were used to try and control them. When more empty tins became available later on, some people experimented with standing the feet of their beds in dishes of water, but the bugs still dropped from the ceilings as soon as the lights were put out. Very few were ever caught, and necks and arms were soon covered in bites. Nor were bugs the only unwelcome visitors – there were lice and fleas in plenty too.

Sister McGauley discovered that their stone cellar floor was less attractive to the bugs than the wooden floor next door. So she and her fellow nuns rather uncharitably pasted strips of paper over the cracks in the connecting door, to make sure that their Benedictine neighbours kept their bugs to themselves!

The spare tins from Red Cross parcels became prized possessions, useful for innumerable purposes. A small group of elderly men formed a little workshop, and devised pots and pans with wire or string handles, grills, mugs and other utensils for anyone who asked. So when the time came to leave for Vittel, many internees walked off to the trains with these clanking and rattling appendages – 'traps' as Aunt Fan called them. Wherever they were being taken, nobody wished to repeat the horrors of their first few ill-equipped meals at Besançon.

Once the Red Cross began to campaign about the conditions in the camp, the internees discovered that a small shower block had started to function. Two French POWs, Marcel and Gaston, were detailed to operate it, and managed to get the boiler going so there was hot water for a precious interval each day. A rota system was developed, organised by the Russian aristocrat Sofka Skipwith, and many of the women made use of this relatively private alternative to public washing in their rooms. Although she was only a self-appointed chief of the *douches*, there seems to be no evidence that anybody ever disputed Sofka's right to organise the rotas. Perhaps her lineage lent her a natural air of authority. Having established how many in each room wanted to use the showers, she allocated the times accordingly and ensured, with the help of the two friendly POWs, that no one outstayed their precisely-allotted time. Sofka in particular was delighted with the new hot water supply, and made sure she had a quick wash each day 'after hours'. But there were so few showers that most people could only have one or two brief turns a month, and besides, many English ladies were not impressed. Aunt Fan took one look and decided they were not for her! She was proud nevertheless that she managed to avoid taking any of the thousands of Besançon bed bugs with her when moving to Vittel.

No sooner had some semblance of order been established, than the inmates of the camp began to change. Some were liberated through ill-health, extreme old age, or because they had left young children at home and were eligible for release under new regulations. Samuel and Elizabeth Hales were released together in early 1941 after a doctor certified that Samuel's heart was weak and he was suffering from bronchitis. The French police in Paris, who were most sympathetic, returned the keys to their flat, and they were allowed to go home, provided they signed on at the police station each day. Rita Harding's mother, on the other hand, was sent home against her wishes because her youngest daughter, aged eleven, was deemed too young to remain in the camp. Meanwhile, new prisoners arrived and had to be squashed into the already crowded rooms. Aunt Fan soon heard that another fifteen women would be coming in, doubling their numbers. This news was not greeted with enthusiasm:

> We were told that we must have beds one on top of another, but we decided against that, but simply put them close together, very close, with just enough space to move. And we waited for the other people to arrive. They told us afterwards that they came from Brittany, and they had been ages on the journey, and they said we looked 'as black as ink' at them, because we didn't want more people in our room! And so these poor wretches had to do what they could, and when they got a stove it smoked, and smoked us out, so we didn't like that. But of course after a day or 2 we all settled down. But we did keep very much apart. The people from Brittany were all English, and in my part of the room they were more French – either the wives of English jockeys, or other wives of Englishmen. Their husbands had escaped to England, leaving these women with their children, thinking that they would not be taken. But they were. And very wretched they were, the mothers who had left their children behind. But we settled down, more or less.

Some of the new arrivals were from as far away as Poland, and seemed to have been rounded up at random, but the great majority were 'British', no matter how tenuous their links with the British Isles really were. Many could barely speak a word of English, and all corners of the globe were

'Nun.'

represented. Some bitterly resented being labelled as British, and could not understand why they had been interned.

One of the consequences of the fluctuating numbers of internees was that beds were constantly being added or removed from rooms. This was done by details of soldiers, who would appear unannounced to make the changes; since coal was strictly rationed, and wood was in short supply, the attractions of an idle wooden bed or two were obvious. Aunt Fan's room had somehow got hold of a saw, which they managed to keep hidden for such occasions, while Sofka Skipwith and her circle of younger women had stolen an axe, smuggled out of a shed inside an army great coat. Sofka's group prided themselves on being able to dismantle, chop up and hide all traces of a bed in ten minutes from the moment the previous occupant left the room. It was then an easy matter to convince the Germans that it had already been removed by another squad of soldiers.

On one occasion, Sofka was nearing the head of the long queue for coal, when the soldier in charge was momentarily called away. She quickly stuffed a handful of coal coupons into an inner pocket, and for a while after that (with careful management) her room had plenty of fuel for their stove.

Among the internees were about 500 nuns from literally dozens of different Orders and Congregations. Sister McGauley counted ninety separate groups. These women, some of whom were from enclosed Orders, some nurses or teachers, did their best to continue their normal occupations while adapting to their situation:

There was a wonderful spirit of comradeship in the camp. What with that and a sense of humour we managed to survive very cheerfully. It was great fun meeting up with everybody in the queues.

On Christmas Day when the Germans were celebrating, word went round the camp that they had forgotten to lock the coal house. It was great fun – everybody filling their buckets over and over again and hiding it under our beds. It was awful really ...

We also stole potatoes when possible. My companions started having scruples so I went to confession and said "Father, I've been stealing potatoes!" and he answered "Très bien ma soeur, continuez!" [Well done, sister, keep it up!]

We stole whenever possible. The Good Shepherds were lucky to wear scapulars which hid a lot!

But the grim reality of their position as prisoners was never far away:

Shortly before we left the camp a rumour was going around that Mother St Chad (a Franciscan Missionary of Mary) who attempted to give classes to the children was in trouble and had been sent for by the Kommandant. We heard no more and in any case were so busy preparing to move camp that it was only after we arrived in Vittel that we realised that she was no longer with us. It was some fifty years later when I heard the full story. I went to Cold Ash to make my retreat and I asked one of her Community for news of her. I have no idea what she must have been up to but I imagine that it was political. On the morning in question she had received some sort of communication from somebody and almost immediately a German soldier came to escort her to the Kommandant. As they were crossing the barracks square she put her hand into her pocket slits, withdrew the communication and shredded it, and when asked for the communication by the Kommandant it was scattered to the four winds.

Mother St Chad was taken to prison and was very ill-treated for years. Finally her brother used his influence to get her over to the Spanish Embassy where she taught English for a while. Eventually she returned to England and although she kept up a close relationship with her Convent she could never return to the religious life after all that she had suffered.

There undoubtedly were links with the underground and resistance movements, from the very early days of the camp. Internees became friendly with those French POWs who were able to come and go more freely, including Marcel and Gaston who ran the shower boiler, and these men gladly ran errands such as posting letters. So did some of the local workmen, the plumbers and electricians, who faced severe punishment if they were caught. Many of Aunt Fan's original pictures were smuggled out in this way, and sent home to Ciboure. The nuns from the city, who helped in the infirmary, took many uncensored letters out, concealed in the hems of their habits, and other local people were willing to help in whatever way they could. The camp medical inspector, Dr Lelong, was occasionally able to arrange a visit into the Bâtiments, and he too sometimes came or went with contraband items.

By whatever means, some internees managed to make contact with at least one shopkeeper who was in an underground organisation in Besançon. The prisoners were helped in smaller ways too, down to shopkeepers slipping extra items like Aunt Fan's map, or slabs of chocolate, into their bags on their rare visits into the city later in the year. There was a profound feeling of gratitude among all those internees who were aware of the risks these local people ran for them.

Some internees also escaped, or tried to do so. Some were helped by the workmen and plumbers building the new toilets; several smuggled themselves into the hollow seats of the van which took visitors to the patients at the city hospital; and others just took their own chances. Often these attempts ended in failure, and then the inmates would hear heavy footfalls and slamming of doors as an escapee was returned to the barracks and locked up. It was understood that in these cases the recaptured internee had already spent some time confined in the prison at the Citadel up on the rocky hill above the town centre; the Citadel that Aunt Fan could see from her window.

One day, Fernande and her friend Hélène found a verse scribbled on the walls of a cell in the prison, written long before by a young soldier:

> Quand les corbeaux seront blancs,
> Et que la neige tombera noire,
> Les souvenirs de VAUBAN
> S'effaceront de ma memoire

> [Only when crows are white
> And snow falls black,
> Will the memories of Vauban
> Fade from my mind.]

That summarised the camp at Besançon, with its filth, its carrion birds picking over the piles of rubbish and waste, its freezing conditions and almost continuous snow, all in a topsy-turvy senseless world.

The weather continued bad for so long, many degrees below the seasonal norm even for this cold corner of France, that the Germans issued the heavy, moth-eaten army-surplus greatcoats and breeches that had been left behind in the barracks. Some were believed to date back to the Franco-Prussian War. Although far from elegant, the coats were thick and quite warm, and were worn continuously on the coldest days, and put on the beds at night. Some enterprising mothers cut them up and made them into clothes for their young children. For footwear, there was a choice of old French army-issue boots or sandals made from their soles (or pieces of wood), with sections of belt for straps. These latter made a constant loud clatter as the wearers came up and down the stone staircases.

Yet the camp was not all bad. The townspeople managed to bring in Christmas presents for many of the smallest children, even though the Germans made no attempt to provide better food on the day, as Aunt Fan rather tartly commented:

> Two of us went hopefully to the shed ... but only came back with the usual. Perhaps supper, we thought? But supper was no better; instead of jam there was a spoonful of lard! Good of its kind, but depressing. I put my spoonful on my shoes.

'Camp guards.'

Various people organised classes for the children, and even managed to put on a junior theatre performance, which was attended by the Kommandant. The teaching nuns worked hard for the benefit of the children, and a Scout group was set up for the older boys. Some of the adults made good use of their time by finding tutors and starting to learn new languages. Fernande, being a professional needlewoman, was able to keep herself very busy. She made embroidered mats and other things with thread she had obtained somehow, and washed the ladies' clothes to earn some spare money for the small luxuries that began to appear on the flourishing black market.

Aunt Fan felt she was especially fortunate to enjoy drawing so much. At first, it was almost impossible to find paper of any sort, but once it became possible to get extra items, or smuggle them in, several women in the camp began drawing quite regularly:

I was very lucky, because I managed to get a whole big block of type-writing paper. One of the French soldiers, a prisoner also, got it for me through the workmen. So, as I had pencils and Indian ink, I was very happy drawing. I had no shortage of models. We had no chairs, only benches, so people sat in all sorts of awkward attitudes! or on their beds, or anywhere. I also went out into the yard and the French soldiers were very nice to me. I could draw the horses they had got; big old horses. They used to warn me if a German officer was coming, and I would nip into one of the vans. The horses were used to pull these vans, for collecting food and so on and I always had time to disappear into a van before a German came along, and then I would come out again afterwards. Easy. So I had all the horses to draw as well, and I was well occupied.

Aunt Fan and other artists made copies of some of their sketches as presents for their fellow-internees. Elizabeth Hales, for example, took one of Stella Gumuchian's drawings with her when she left, and May Yates, who shared Aunt Fan's room, was given a booklet of sketches when she was freed in April 1941.

'Our boiler.'

Morale began to improve at Besançon once the postal service started working, many weeks after it should have done. The camp was designated 'Frontstalag 142', a title which it kept until after the transfer to Vittel. Once news of the inmates' whereabouts got out, their families and friends began to write letters. At first, both the internees and their families believed they were able to write normal (sealed) letters, but few of these ever reached their destination, and incoming letters in particular were held up for a long time before being delivered. Then, in January 1941, the Germans issued an order that inmates were to use letter forms, and restrict correspondence to a few sentences, while families were still allowed to send in sealed letters. All these were of course subjected to careful censorship. In March, letters were again permitted, but in an attempt to speed up delivery they were initially limited to two per month in each direction, per inmate. Later this was increased to three letter forms and two postcards a month.

If the mood at Vauban was substantially improved by communication with home, the arrival of the first parcels was a cause of jubilation. Sometimes these came from relations or, in the case of the nuns, from their convents, but conditions in the occupied zone were already harsh for civilians, and there was not much food to spare. The great delight and salvation of many was undoubtedly the Red Cross parcels, which became a highlight of camp life. It is no exaggeration to say that the contents of these parcels saved many inmates' lives. The first batch arrived at the end of January, and after that their arrival was an occasional but hugely appreciated event. After relying entirely on the terrible German rations for so many weeks, there was paradise in these parcels with their precious tea and powdered milk, chocolate, soap, biscuits, tinned meat and, of course, the cigarettes that soon became a valuable unit of currency for those, like Aunt Fan, who did not smoke. The delivery of each new set of parcels was an opportunity for fresh experimentation with new recipes, and much swapping of ingredients.

The International Red Cross had first been alerted to the existence of the camp on 11 December 1940, by an aid organisation in Paris. By 17 December, the British Red Cross was in communication with the International Committee about the matter, and contact was made with the German authorities. After some delay, there was a fresh demand for information and access to the internees which met with a more positive response in the middle of January 1941, a full month later than legally expected. A visit was finally arranged for representatives from Switzerland to visit the camp at the end of the month. This eventually paved the way for the various improvements made at Besançon and, ultimately, to the transfer of the prisoners to Vittel. Ironically, the woman at the head of the German Red Cross was Frau Goëring, right from the top

Fernande, Hélène and other internees in their room at Besançon.

echelons of the Nazi party, and she herself came with that first delegation
to Besançon.

However, camp life was not transformed overnight. Despite the greatly
improved diet afforded by the occasional parcels, for most of the time the
camp kitchen remained the main source of food. The few doctors were
always kept busy, and when outbreaks of food poisoning occurred, they
were overwhelmed. On at least one occasion, an incident which killed
dozens of people was attributed to cooked food being left exposed overnight in a copper vat. At other times, infections suddenly swept through
the barrack blocks. Then there would be a rush for the stairs to try and get
out across the courtyard in time. The most elderly prisoners often fell in
their haste, and some, perhaps many, died of exposure in the process, as
Elizabeth Hales recorded in her diary:

We are not without epidemics. In cold snowy weather one night we are all waken up with terrible pains. Some rooms are worse than others. Personally I am obliged to go downstairs to the cabinet 4 times in the night. Sam however does not fall ill. It has to do with the food stuffs. We don't know if the kitchen utensils are kept clean enough. It is a form of poisoning. The young doctors come over from the Infirmary and attend to really bad cases. In Sam's room an old man of 70 goes down several times in snow and on final return journey stumbles across door and falls dead. These illnesses take place twice. Whether intentional or accidental we shall never know.

Strange things happen from time to time. Once a woman commits suicide by jumping out of the window. From time to time we see melancholy groups of people taking over invalids to the Infirmary on stretchers.

Aunt Fan's sister Kathleen was one of the early casualties of the bad food and unsanitary conditions:

She was so ill that we could not get her down the stairs, because the 52 steps down, made of stone, had got very slippery with the water and the snow we had brought in on our feet. We could not do anything with her. So they sent a French doctor, and he had her taken away on a stretcher. I didn't know where she had gone to. In fact, they took her over to the Infirmary and I managed in a day or 2 to get over there and see her. It was in the yard. She was much better there, they had proper beds. The French doctors were very nice, and they did what they could. I fortunately did not get ill. The great fear was falling ill, because with no water in the place and everything frozen, it didn't do to be ill. People looked after each other as well as they could.

From the camp infirmary, there were three ways out. A significant number of the sick died, and a few of these are still buried in unnamed graves. The lucky ones were 'reformed', that is to say they persuaded the doctors and the Germans to release them on health grounds. Some women who had worked as nurses managed to pass off another patient's X-ray results as their own and so were set free. As time went on, more and more of the older and less fit internees were sent home, on more or less genuine medical grounds, with orders to report to their local police every day. Those who were too weak to make the journey home, like Aunt Kathleen, were sent into the city, to the Hôpital St Jacques, an institution which for many years had served the sick, poor and elderly of Besançon.

6

L'Hôpital St Jacques

After three days in the camp infirmary, Aunt Kathleen was transferred to the city hospital, to a ward of sick internees. When she had recovered enough, the Germans told her she was free to make her way home. After her release, she wrote a short description of the hospital, which was later incorporated into the fair copy of her sister's diary.

HOPITAL S^T JACQUES
BY K.T.

The hospital is a very fine old building (1702) partially modernised but more suited for a workhouse infirmary.

The Salle St Bernard was immense, 225 ft. long and about 45 ft. wide. The sills of the very dirty windows were 16 ft. above the floor. The walls were dark, the beds in four rows, the centre double rows only truckle beds as the Germans had removed the good beds. One end of the room, opening on to stone stairs, consisted of wood and glass, at the other end a door led to a small stairway up to various small rooms and upper wards. No passages so there was a constant "through traffic" of everyone and everything.

A passage off the N. end led to the "lavabo" ie. a small room with one tap of hot water and a sink, then up two steps to a narrow room with 3 fixed basins, no plugs and only cold taps. Small enamelled basins had to be filled at the hot tap and balanced on the big basins somehow. A tiled space at the window end had short curtains for "private" washing. The other half of the room was fitted with 2 "W.Cs" namely open holes in white tiled floor with iron half doors in front, no handles, no rail, no means of fastening the half door. These were used by 60-70 women, children and French soldiers – The window was broken so washing was a cold affair in below zero temperatures – I always washed at about

2 AM to avoid the crowd. In the more modern wards these arrangements were better.

Only 8 or 9 among the 70 odd women in this ward were English. There were Polish, Swiss, Armenians, Egyptians and many French wives or daughters of English or naturalised British subjects mostly rather low class. Very few spoke English.

I was lucky to have nice neighbours, an old English governess and then a pleasant woman, the sister of a bank clerk in Paris and on my other side a wooden partition, part of a cubicle where oddments such as curtains were kept which made a kind of corner.

Four big lamps were left alight all night and a sister went round with a lantern at least once each night. The senior sister made a round each morning and spoke to every patient. She was deaf and every answer had to be shouted down her large ear trumpet so there could be no secrets discussed with her.

A nun from a neighbouring hospital came in for an hour or two every day and did all the nursing and dressing beyond the capacities of the patients themselves. The two sisters belonging to each ward had all they could do with their supervision of the cleaning, serving meals, sorting washing and their long hours in chapel.

Medecines came up from the dispensary in a tray, bottles and boxes of pills etc with little scraps of paper on them numbered according to the order of the beds. These labels were taken off to return to the dispenser and the sister handed out a half dozen at a time to anyone willing to carry them round. Why no one was not poisoned I don't know as "strychnine pills for 18" – "cough mixture for 73" or "castor oil for 37" was just carried round and it was difficult to remember who had to have which potion or pill.

Two soldiers, French prisoners, came in and out all day doing the little sweeping we ever saw done, wheeling up the huge food tins and if paid doing little errands for us.

A day in the Hospital –

2 AM – washed in the "lavabo", window broken, temperature some degrees below zero – water warm.

6.30 breakfast "coffee" a brown sweet liquid and bread brought round by French soldiers. On Sundays breakfast was at 5.30.

Made beds, read, worked, helped the sisters sort washing, or roll bandages or take round medecines.

10 AM Dinner, stew, potatoes, lentils, rutabaga by turns, occasionally a spoonful of apple sauce, carried round on trollies and ladled into each plate. Only room for about 30 at the table so I had my meals by my bed.

Also had each ¼ pint of wine. Washed plate, knife, fork and spoon at the only tap. Then visited friends in other wards or walked in the cloisters or the small bit of garden.

4 PM tisane, in big cans taken round.

5 PM supper. soup and bread supplemented with contents of red cross parcels.

8 PM Lights out except for four centre globes.

As I could not manage the "stew" of rice, lentils etc, all cooked without salt in a watery mess, the sister usually produced a roast potato from her pocket and this was solemnly presented and duly received with much gratitude on my part and a grin from the sisters. Neighbours were always ready for my share of the "stew".

What Aunt Kathleen did not mention in this account, but noted in a letter written to her sister Dora in England soon afterwards, was that there were a further three women, one boy of seventeen and a five-year-old foundling in the ward, all of whom were insane and presumably very noisy as a result. There were also large communal buckets, one for every five or six beds, for those who could not get as far as the WCs. A second large ward was set aside for men, and the third housed 127 children and teenagers.

As her health improved and she was able to walk, Kathleen was allowed outside into the garden and cloisters of the front courtyard, but to her amusement she was always accompanied by a guard. Her convalescence went well until one day she fell on the frozen snow and damaged her arm, which then took weeks to recover.

Kathleen's surviving letter suggests that her six-week stay in the hospital, and her eventual journey home, were relatively pleasant, although this was perhaps merely to reassure her relatives in England:

The supper which we had at 5 pm was a soup made with vermicelli or barley and bread, with a small bit of cheese, apple stew or prunes (with no sugar) for non meat-eaters, also rice and macaroni. I had a baked potato most days as the stew did not agree. The dispensary sister did the dressings and such nursing as was beyond the patient's neighbours in bed. There were two sisters in the ward on duty the whole day, always. One walked round at night with a lantern and could be called if needed. Their devotion and patient kindness was beyond description.

I left the hospital on 26th February, leaving Fanny in the camp. We had a good journey in a new second class carriage for Biarritz with 18 others. 3 stopped in Paris, 1 at Bayonne, 14 for Biarritz. There were also 2 German nurses and a doctor going for a holiday there. V. Dugdale & I then had the whole compartment to ourselves. Hot 'coffee' or soup was given 3 times & a bread & margarine sandwich the 2nd day. There was snow on the ground till Paris. Left Besançon at 10.30 am, reached Paris about 11 pm & St Jean de Luz at 8 pm on Thursday 27th.

There was a south wind and flowers in bloom.

For Kathleen, now aged sixty-one, the internment was over, but in Besançon the war was only just beginning.

Although the German military were not aware of the fact for many months, the Hôpital St Jacques was not merely a neutral infirmary where they could rid themselves of responsibility for sick internees. From the outset of the occupation, it was also at the heart of the resistance movement in the region.

The original hospital at Besançon had been founded outside the old city walls in the twelfth century by the Madeleine Sisters as a 'hospice' offering overnight accommodation for pilgrims. By the sixteenth century, it had passed to another Order, which cared mainly for the poor. It was then taken over by the City Fathers, who decided to build a new medical facility within the walls to replace the outmoded and dilapidated old hospice. But the dedication to St James, St Jacques in French, the patron of pilgrims, was retained. Work on the new hospital began in 1672, and the first patients were admitted in 1691. In its time, l'Hôpital St Jacques was known as one of the finest hospitals in France, caring for the poor as well as the sick. It was staffed by doctors from the university medical faculty and nuns from the Hôtel Dieu (a uniquely French institution combining the functions of pilgrim hospice and hospital) at Beaune, 100 km to the west, who served as nurses. A pharmacist was also appointed to set up and run a state-of-the-art dispensary.

The buildings were arranged around three courtyards. The main court, for patients, was surrounded on three sides by covered walkways reminiscent of a cloister, and open on the fourth side to the road through imposing wrought-iron gates. A central open-plan chapel on the first floor landing was arranged so the patients could follow the services from their beds when the big wooden doors at the ends of the wards were open. These first floor wards, each dedicated to a patron saint, were deliberately built with high windows and ceilings to reduce the risk of draughts reaching the beds. As well as the central staircase, there were other stairs at the far ends of the wards, and on the ground floor there were many small rooms, some reserved for the use of the nuns. Although from the outside it seemed rather an austere building, l'Hôpital St Jacques had been carefully designed as a model eighteenth-century hospital; coincidentally, it also lent itself very well to clandestine operations. There were few dead-ends, plenty of escape routes, and innumerable places to hide.

The pharmacy was central to the role of the hospital in the Resistance. From 1666, when the first committee began planning the new hospital, it was always intended to have a pharmacist working there. The first Master Apothecary was Gabriel Gaston (1612-92), one of the greatest practitioners of the time. Under his guidance, a fully stocked and beautifully furnished pharmacy was built, which began functioning in the new hospital as soon as it opened. It still survives, with rows and rows of elegant little enamelled containers: more than 240 pots, miniature bottles and covered jugs, 200 tiny boxes, sets of scales and dozens of utensils. During the war, this was still in use as the hospital pharmacy, under the control of Sister Marcelle Baverez.

Sister Baverez was born in Besançon in 1899, and served her noviciate there, training in many different branches of nursing. After several years away from the city broadening her expertise, she returned to take charge of the pharmacy at l'Hôpital St Jacques shortly before the war. All the departments of the hospital quickly became involved in an efficient network for the reception, safe-keeping and transmission of all those evading capture. The pharmacy, with its innumerable places where notes and messages could be safely hidden, was at its heart, but the rooms and staff of the laundry, kitchens, administration rooms and even the maternity unit were all part of the system. Sister Broihier, in charge of the morgue, played a particularly prominent role, smuggling people in and out of the hospital grounds in coffins and hearses.

At first, the emphasis of the underground operations at l'Hôpital St Jacques was on Allied and French soldiers evading capture at the time of the armistice. Almost 2,000 of the troops held at Besançon were hospitalised and many of these were spirited away to the south. Later, attention turned to escaped POWs and allies on the run in France, whether clandestine agents or pilots who had been shot down over occupied territories. Whatever their need, the hospital was a clearing house for the movement of these men and occasionally women towards the border with the unoccupied zone. So while Kathleen and her fellow patients convalesced, the work of repatriation and liberation of wanted people was going on right under the noses of their German guards.

Each day, Sister Baverez made a habit of sending up medicines for the patients, carefully labelled on the scraps of paper which Aunt Kathleen commented on with such amusement. But the pharmacist also sent up messages for some of the patients, or brought them herself on her visits to the wards when she came to assist with the nursing, as Kathleen sometimes saw her doing. These messages came from the Resistance, or were about arrangements for escapes. A typical plan would be that at a given time, a 'patient' would get up and dress in clothes supplied by the sisters, and his place in the bed would be taken by one of the staff. Three days after he had left the building, the Germans would be notified that an escape had just taken place. This strategy had a high success rate, simply by concentrating the resulting search in the immediate vicinity of the hospital. The reporting of escapes also helped to reduce suspicion that the staff were themselves involved.

French citizens were sometimes helped too. Just as the POW doctors at Caserne Vauban tried to get internees registered as medically unfit so that they could be sent home, so the staff of l'Hôpital St Jacques could prescribe drugs to induce symptoms which might relieve Frenchmen of the dreaded forced labour imposition, and Sister Baverez sometimes supplied papers which enabled them to move to the unoccupied zone.

By 1943, however, the net was closing. Five of the hospital nursing sisters had been arrested and brutally interrogated by the Gestapo. Eventually, in August 1943, Sister Baverez was caught. She was moved around from camp to camp and interrogated repeatedly, but refused to give the Gestapo the information they demanded. At last, at the end of January 1944 she was sent to Ravensbrück. In August, the camp inmates were vaccinated simultaneously against typhoid, diphtheria and typhus, but she was so malnourished by then that it killed her. She died in November 1944, after a long and painful illness, watched over by a Protestant nun with whom she had been imprisoned for many months. The community at the Besançon hospital only heard of her fate in April the following year.

Besançon itself was liberated in September 1944, while Sister Baverez remained imprisoned. L'Hôpital St Jacques was immediately inundated with German prisoners, many of whom were terribly sick. This was one of the greatest tests of the calibre and calling of the nuns. In the words of their Mother Superior, they put the past behind them and obeyed the commandment to return good for evil.

7

Vittel: The Golden Cage

With both the Red Cross and the British Government working on behalf of the internees, conditions gradually improved a little at Besançon. Eventually, however, it may have been a direct threat, originating it was believed with Churchill himself, which produced the desired effect. Word was thought to have reached those in authority in Germany that if something radical was not done about the conditions at Frontstalag 142, the German civilians interned in Britain would be moved to the north of Canada, through the waters where the Battle of the Atlantic was raging. (In fact a secret policy of this sort, whereby German POWs were deported to Canada, had already been operating for some time on security grounds, and as early as June 1940 the SS *Duchess of York* had also transported 2,100 internees).

Early in April 1941, Lieutenant Otto Landhauser came to the spa town of Vittel, some 120 km north of Besançon, to assess the amount of accommodation in the numerous hotels. He told the mayor of Vittel that a 'camp' was to be set up for German women. On his second visit, he informed the mayor, M. Jean Bouloumié, that it was in fact to be an internment camp for the British women from Besançon. The town thus had some notice of the arrival of the internees, and Landhauser, soon to be promoted Captain, was able to prepare for his role as Kommandant.

In Besançon, meanwhile, there was no hint of the impending move until the day when the first batch of inmates, in Bâtiment A, were told they were to go to the showers and have all their possessions fumigated. Bâtiment C, where Aunt Fan and Sister McGauley were housed, was one of the last buildings to be evacuated, so its residents had ample time to observe what was going on elsewhere. The nuns in particular were unhappy at the way it was to be done:

Our conditions had been pronounced sub human by the Red Cross and we were to be moved out in May. Towards the end of April we were told that we were to be de-bugged very shortly before moving to another Camp. We were to strip naked leaving our clothes and belongings behind and go across the square draped only in a blanket to have a shower in the infirmary quarters. There was an uproar in the Camp! Looking out of our window towards the infirmary an army of soldiers was trying to control the riot. We could see Mother Ste Augustine from Bayeux (she spoke fluent German) talking to a German officer. Finally it was agreed that the religious should take a solitary bath whilst our clothes were disinfected and we were to sleep the night in the infirmary. Sister Mary Catherine and I were shown into a room with four beds in it ... We were soon joined by seven others so we were nine people of seven different Congregations and only four beds! We didn't even have those baths after all, they were too filthy.

Whilst so many soldiers were out trying to restore order they had left the coal house unattended on the other side of the barracks square and prisoners from here, there and everywhere were making off with the coal.

Mabel Bayliss was one of those involved in the protest:

On a certain day orders were given to have the luggage ready for 11.30 pm. We had heard much noise and movement going on, eventually at 2 am the Germans came. By torch light we had to carry our luggage to the infirmary, where it was to be disinfected. Each valise was opened, one piled on the top of the other and it sounded like a 'Hoover' working in the room – a mere comedy. The luggage, some valises broken, was returned; we had to bundle our things in the best way we could and carry it to a higher floor.

At five in the morning we were ordered to strip, give our clothes to be disinfected, wrap ourselves in our bed blanket and go to the shower-bath across the courtyard. As regards stripping, we went on a silent strike. Early in the morning hundreds of women stood silently before the Kommandatur, the Heads carried our demand to the Commander. No satisfactory answer was given and we were ordered to return to our respective barracks at once; not a woman budged and then the sentries appeared as if they had orders to fire. One woman, seeing a gun raised by a German, pushed him back. This action called for real imprisonment and she disappeared for a long period. A sentry fired – a blank shot – but the noise was sufficient to send the majority back to the rooms! We finally went to the baths, undressed there, gave our clothes to the black Colonial French prisoner to take to be disinfected and sat there wrapped in a khaki blanket until they returned. Many of us, objecting to undressing in the awful crowd, just made a bundle of our top garments and pretended to take a shower. After dressing, we queued up in the dusky morning and after waiting a lengthy time we were conducted to the train that was to take us to our unknown destiny. It seemed as though the train would never leave Besançon. Three times we returned in view of the barracks and could hear the cheers of those waiting their turn to undergo disinfection!

It was only about 200 km by train from Besançon to Vittel, but the journey took two days. The women were cold, weary and bedraggled when finally they arrived on the first of May. There had been no official notification of their destination, even though the German authorities had known for a month where they were going to be moved. As a result, few people were able to tell their families where they were going or why, and the Red Cross parcels which should have reached them in Besançon ceased to arrive, making them all once more dependent on the inadequate German rations. The final insult was that as the women were hustled into their hotels, a crowd of photographers jostled round, taking pictures which must have looked good in subsequent propaganda images of the luxurious quarters arranged for the British internees. Many deliberately looked away as the photographs were taken.

On entering the hotels, the women were frightened to look in the elegant gilt-framed mirrors and see reflected back images of gaunt, dishevelled beings, strangers in their own eyes.

Aunt Fan was housed in room 212 of The Grand Hotel with Mrs Trotter, whom she had got to know at Besançon.

Although the British Red Cross had temporarily lost touch with the internees, the French Committee was very much involved. Mme Germaine Bouloumié had recently been appointed President of the Vittel Red Cross, and she was determined to see that the camp was decently and legally run. In addition to her Red Cross role, she also worked as the official link between

Mme Bouloumié.

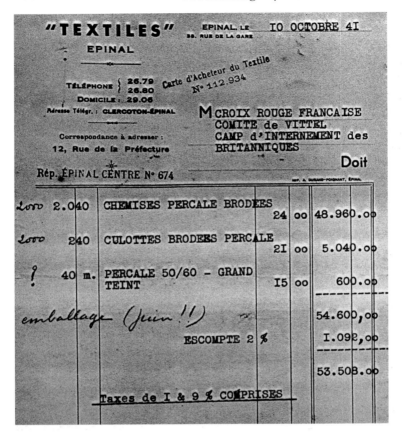

"TEXTILES"   EPINAL, LE   IO OCTOBRE 41
                  35, RUE DE LA GARE

  EPINAL

TÉLÉPHONE { 26.79   Carte d'Acheteur du Textile
             26.80   N° 112.934
DOMICILE : 29.06
Adresse Télégr. : CLERCOTON-ÉPINAL   M CROIX ROUGE FRANCAISE
                                        COMITE de VITTEL
Correspondance à adresser :   CAMP d'INTERNEMENT des
12, Rue de la Préfecture   BRITANNIQUES

                                                        Doit
Rép. ÉPINAL CENTRE N° 674
                                        IMP. A. DURAND-POIGNANT, ÉPINAL.

	2.040	CHEMISES PERCALE BRODÉES	24	00	48.960.00
	240	CULOTTES BRODÉES PERCALE	21	00	5.040.00
?	40 m.	PERCALE 50/60 - GRAND TEINT	15	00	600.00
		emballage (Juin!!)			54.600,00
		ESCOMPTE 2 %			1.092,00
					53.508.00

Taxes de I & 9 % COMPRISES

Above and below: Red Cross orders for clothing for the internees at Vittel.

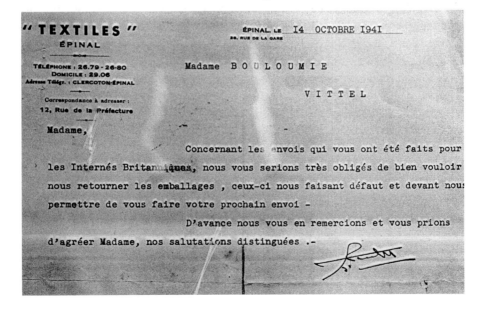

"TEXTILES"   ÉPINAL, LE   I4 OCTOBRE I94I
                  35, RUE DE LA GARE

ÉPINAL

TÉLÉPHONE : 26.79 - 26-80   Madame B O U L O U M I E
DOMICILE : 29.06
Adresse Télégr. : CLERCOTON-ÉPINAL   V I T T E L

Correspondance à adresser :
12, Rue de la Préfecture

Madame,

          Concernant les envois qui vous ont été faits pour
les Internés Britanniques, nous vous serions très obligés de bien vouloir
nous retourner les emballages , ceux-ci nous faisant défaut et devant nous
permettre de vous faire votre prochain envoi -

          D'avance nous vous en remercions et vous prions
d'agréer Madame, nos salutations distinguées .-

the other aid organisations, notably the YMCA, and the German authorities. It was largely due to her efforts that conditions for the internees became relatively comfortable, and that international laws were obeyed. In her report presented soon after liberation in September 1944, she noted that on their arrival the prisoners were extremely poorly dressed, largely in discarded army uniforms and boots. With the consent of Captain Landhauser, Mme Bouloumié purchased 300 pairs of shoes, 1,000 pairs of stockings, 10,000 metres of material, and large quantities of underwear for both men and women to supply their immediate needs. Thereafter, she insisted on making at least one official fortnightly visit to the camp, to try and hear the internees' requests and complaints and to meet them as far as possible.

Another personal touch, arranged by the YMCA and the Red Cross, was to get a local photographer to come into the camp and take pictures of groups of the internees so they could send them home. This was a popular idea, and many of the surviving internees still have these photographs among their treasured possessions.

The camp was established around the central park and the thermal springs, which in kinder days were at the heart of the spa town. The nuns were mostly put into the Continental Hotel, near a small chapel, while the other internees were spread among the Grand Hotel, the Vittel Palace, the Cérès, and some rooms of the Casino. The whole area, including part of the park, was fenced off with lines of high barbed wire. As more internees were moved to Vittel – an initial instalment of about 300 Americans in October 1942 for example – more hotels were pressed into service. These Americans had been arrested earlier in the year, in much the same way as the British had been in 1940, and many had spent some time in newly constructed wooden barracks blocks at Besançon before being transferred to Vittel. When large numbers of Jews, many from Poland, were held at Vittel in 1943 and 1944, a new enclave was made for them, linked to the park by a walkway over the road. At its maximum, about 3,000 people were held in the camp.

Although the prisoners were now housed in hotels not barracks, it would be wrong to imagine that their lives were anything approaching luxurious. Compared with Besançon, certainly, it seemed to be paradise. A lucky few had individual rooms, or at worst they shared one between four or six, and most rooms had a basin and easy access to a lavatory. The beds were good, and there were real sheets! Apart from all this, the bitter winter was finally coming to an end, it was spring and there was free access to the park in the middle of the day. But all the carpets and most curtains had been removed – the hotels had been empty for a year apart from some POWs in transit – temperatures continued to fall below freezing at night for several weeks, there was no heating, and the rations were at first nearly

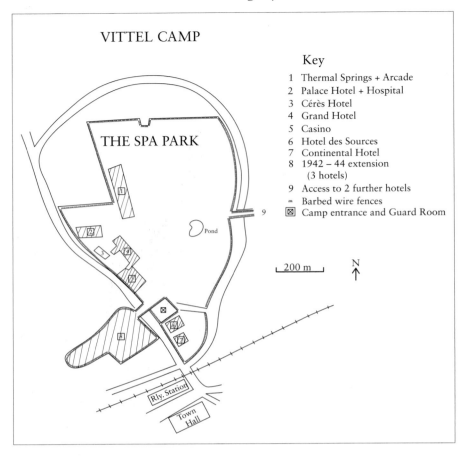

VITTEL CAMP

Key

1 Thermal Springs + Arcade
2 Palace Hotel + Hospital
3 Cérès Hotel
4 Grand Hotel
5 Casino
6 Hotel des Sources
7 Continental Hotel
8 1942 – 44 extension
  (3 hotels)
9 Access to 2 further hotels
▪ Barbed wire fences
☒ Camp entrance and Guard Room

THE SPA PARK

Pond

200 m

N

Rly. Station

Town Hall

as bad as at Besançon. In those wartime winters at Vittel, the water did not merely freeze on the window panes at night, but also in mugs in the rooms.

Before long, however, conditions began to improve. The regular visits and dedicated work of Mme Bouloumié ensured that the Red Cross parcels started to arrive again, and hot water began to flow intermittently in the taps. The other rights of the internees – to a canteen, entertainment and so on – were also now respected. And once there was some boiling water for making drinks, supplied from the 'cuisine roulante' (a mobile camp boiler), morale drastically improved.

The health of the internees was soon transformed. Being able to keep clean, and having better food and more comfortable conditions made a great difference. Instead of the crude and rat-infested military-style camp kitchen of Besançon, the rations were prepared (albeit still by a military cook) in the hotel kitchens.

One of the hotels at the edge of the park, The Vittel Palace, was turned into a hospital. It was staffed by a group of twenty Marianite Nursing Sisters, who slept and worked on site. There were also, at different times, nine POW doctors: seven French (one a Jew, Dr Levi) and two Scotsmen. They organised regular health check-ups and were always available for consultations, going out of their way to help their fellow prisoners. The Red Cross arranged that these doctors, and a group of seventy French African POWs, should be allowed permanent passes for access into the town in order to obtain supplies; they were thus able to facilitate some illicit errands for the internees. The medical staff was helped by volunteers from among the internees, including Rita Harding, who worked in the hospital administration office.

The Red Cross parcels began to be delivered again at the end of June, after a two month delay, and once more became central to the internees' lives. Rationing was increasingly severe for civilians in France, and the contents of the parcels caused considerable envy among the men who came into the camp to work on the heating and plumbing. Some places were eventually identified where the barbed-wire perimeter was less securely guarded, and exchanges could take place. Fresh vegetables and eggs from Vittel were pushed through, and cigarettes, tins and dried food were collected; when the French civilians were caught, they faced a severe beating, or worse. Many good things also found their way into the hands of the French workmen, who were often willing to try and smuggle messages or parcels out of the camp. It also did not go unnoticed that the parcels greatly annoyed the German officers, who were busy trying to convince their captives that Britain was being starved into surrender, and would soon capitulate.

The archives of the Vittel Red Cross reveal that each of their parcels contained between sixteen and twenty items (always including tea and soap), from the following basic list of two dozen: 2 ounces of tea, two small tins of sugar, one tablet of soap, ½ lb margarine, one tin of paté, one tin of tomatoes, ¼ lb slab of chocolate, milk (either powder or a tin of condensed), one packet or tin of biscuits, one tin of stewed meat and vegetables, one packet of Ovaltine or cocoa, Beemax (a fortified flour as a vitamin B1 supplement, concentrated from wheat-germ, which came either in a box or in the form of a fruit pasty), one tinned pudding weighing about a pound, one tin of jam, one small pot of meat paste, one tin of cheese, half a packet of rice, three sausages or four to six rashers of bacon, one packet of sweets, ½ lb of dried fruit, one medium box of salmon or herrings, one small pot of mustard, one small pot of curry, ¼ lb of coffee, one tiny box of Yeatex (a vitamin B supplement made from yeast).

One parcel per internee, delivered every week on a Friday; they were indeed an 'unfailing delight'. The variation between the parcels, as well as personal preferences, ensured there was plenty of scope for swapping and trading. Much of this trade was carried on with cigarettes, which were supplied separately through the Red Cross. Notice boards also appeared: 'Tea wanted; I offer 1 lb dates'. '2 tins of condensed milk wanted, for sugar; room 212.'

Some people had additional private parcels from home, but those with relatives or friends in France found that food supplies were becoming more difficult for those outside than for the inmates of the camp with their Red Cross support:

By this time we were receiving regular British Red Cross parcels. We also received parcels from home [in England] every three months. People were advised to send soap and chocolate ... not a very good combination! The parcels were so long en route that the chocolate was quite inedible.

Revd Mother General used to write and say "Je vous en prie, achetez des haricots!" [I beg you, buy us some beans!] I don't know where she used to think that we could buy them from? Sentinels at the gate, a great barbed wire fence all round the camp, and beyond that a few yards on, no-man's-land surrounded yet again by another barbed wire fence with sentinels on the March beyond that!

True, there was a small canteen in the camp which sometimes sold gingerbread but it meant queuing for hours which was too exhausting. We did receive 300 francs a month from the Red Cross but we had no means of spending it ... and eventually it was stolen by the Germans. The Red Cross also supplied us with shoes when required.

Later on, things became scarce even in the relatively well-provisioned Vittel camp. The nuns tried hard to maintain their standards, but it was not easy:

Mother St Benedict gave us calligraphy classes. We had no pens, but used sticks of firewood shaped at the end like nibs. It was alright for notices! ... We all did a certain amount of cleaning with no cleaning materials other than elbow grease. One of my jobs was to scrub our corridor ... Soap was very scarce – we gathered all the scraps, put them in a rag and dipped them in boiling water and so made balls of soap.

Angers [the home convent] sent us starch made from chestnuts for our coifs but we didn't really have the facilities or the know how. Finally another sister offered to do them for us.

There was an old range in the cellar which used to be lit and on which our buckets of washing (with or without soap) vied with each other to get to the centre of the stove and eventually boil ...

Mabel Bayliss vividly remembered getting the 300 francs, the official prisoner-of-war allowance. In addition, up to 600 francs a month was allowed in from the outside world. When money was going to be dealt out, notices were put up and everyone on the list had to assemble and then wait around while it was doled out in alphabetical order. This could take a whole day.

The 'canteen' was run by a lady called Rosie. Before the war, she had run a fashion boutique in Paris, and at Vittel she adapted her expertise to running a small general store selling any items she could that were not available from the Red Cross: reels of cotton, tissues or paper. Her stocks varied somewhat according to the time of year and depending on what her various suppliers could offer. The bakery items were especially popular, as were the fresh fruit and vegetables from gardens that some of the internees cultivated in the park. Rosie also worked in the Kommandant's office in the mornings, and there she kept her ears open for any hints of trouble brewing, which she could pass on to those involved. One of her suppliers in the town was fully trusted by the Germans, who believed that he was a collaborator, while in fact he was a staunch member of the local underground. As time went on, these contacts became increasingly important for the internees who remained in the camp.

Life at Vittel was better organised than at Caserne Vauban. The internees knew what to expect, knew what they had to do, and of course the conditions were so much better that more was possible. From the start, classes were organised for the children, and as far as possible they followed a normal school curriculum. There were also numerous occupations for the adults, from painting, singing and acting, to bridge clubs, book-binding courses (taught by Aunt Fan), and some serious language and literature classes, helped by the growing library. The Quakers supplied a large number of books, and these were supplemented by spare volumes from the inmates, and by donations from other aid

'A Crested Tit.'

organisations. Some people, it is true, gradually sank into apathy, just waiting for the war to be over, barely listening to the news brought into the camp by the workmen; but many did what they could, and contributed what skills they had. Even if an activity seemed mindless, it was better than doing nothing. Sister McGauley found a use for everything:

> I used to unravel the coarse string from our Red Cross parcels and make yards of fine plaits. I made table centres ... the final result looked like fine crochet work.

Fernande was able to turn her professional skills to good effect:

> At London where I was born, I was a dress designer with Norman Hartnell, so in order to earn a little money I took up my work again and did dressmaking for the internees. At first I had to do everything by hand, but then one day I discovered a sewing machine at the back of one of the shops in the spa arcade. The shop was called 'Chez Barclay'. After getting permission, I took over the premises and set up in business! I had plenty of customers, and no time to be bored.

The Gumuchians at Vittel, seated from the right: Stella, Sonia (holding a bag she made with scraps of string) and their mother. These photographs were taken by a studio in Vittel once conditions had improved in the camp, so the internees had pictures to send home.

Performances in the Casino, of concerts, recitals, and eventually complete variety shows and theatre productions, gradually became more and more elaborate, encouraged by Stella Gumuchian who ran a thriving orchestra using instruments brought into the camp by the Red Cross. Folk dances of the allied and occupied nations were very popular, and enthusiastically enjoyed, but for some reason Mendelssohn's music was forbidden. Costumes were more problematic than arranging a programme and learning the parts, but with ingenuity and careful planning a great deal could be achieved using cardboard, old Red Cross packaging, bed linen, and a bit of imagination.

While she was at Vittel, Aunt Fan became friendly with a lady called Lucy Cashman, who was interned with her husband and who, like her, was approaching sixty. It was perhaps through Mrs Cashman that Aunt Fan came to know the Gumuchian sisters, since they had a shared interest in music; Mrs Cashman was one of two cellists in the camp, Sonia Gumuchian played the accordion and her sister Stella was a violinist. At the time of Aunt Fan's release, arrangements were being finalised for a display of all the arts and crafts work done in the camp. According to the schedule for this exhibition, which was held four days after her release, three of Aunt Fan's pictures were entered for her, two by Lucy Cashman and a third by another friend, a Mrs Lord.

As well as events arranged by the internees, the Casino was used by the camp officials as the venue for regular showings of films on Saturdays and Sundays. Some were good, but many were mere propaganda, often of a crudely anti-Semitic nature. The more politically active of the internees organised boycotts of these.

Many people took part in the various gymnastics and games clubs in the first summer, organised by Miss Stanley, a games mistress in her mid-twenties. She had already tried to organise some sports at Besançon, with the limited facilities available, and now she was able to achieve much more. There were some tennis courts at the far end of the camp, near the perimeter wire, and a few people who had managed to obtain rackets even played there for a while. For the others, there was netball, volley ball, table tennis, hockey and a whole series of dancing and keep-fit classes, including some for the older women, which Mabel Bayliss attended:

This gymnastic teacher started a class for the 'rheumatic' age, over forties. At the end of the class we all had to lie sideways on our backs, then she would suddenly shout "Somersault backwards". We poor old things, fat and thin, usually with shrieks of laughter, got our legs stuck up in the air and rolled over sideways.

Miss Stanley was one of the internees who was least willing to accept the petty tyrannies of the camp regime. Aunt Fan does not mention why she was sent away, but Stanley's friends knew. One day in October 1941 when a Red Cross delegation was touring the camp, she broke through the protective ranks to protest that many of their cigarettes were being kept by the Germans for their own use. No sooner had the delegation left, than she was told to pack her bags; she was taken to the Liebenau camp in Germany, with all the dangers implicit in no longer being on French soil. Liebenau was based in an old mental hospital, from which some of the patients had been abruptly and brutally 'removed' to make way for civilian internees. So that was the end of the games clubs. Stanley remained at Liebenau, in conditions more restricted than those at Vittel, until the end of the war.

The Vittel camp continued to be designated Frontstalag 142 for the first few weeks. Then it was temporarily known as Frontstalag 121, and finally from November 1941 it was renumbered 194. Each time it was renamed, it was also transferred to a new administrative region of France and a new system of postage was arranged, with inevitable delays in deliveries. But the restrictions on the numbers of letters the inmates were allowed to send and receive were never removed; four letters and three cards a month was the maximum ever allowed. Why this was so is not clear, when other civilian internment camps had fewer restrictions imposed.

Otto Landhauser served as the Kommandant at Vittel throughout the war, supported by two junior officers: Steffahn, who had a bad temper but was generally quite well-liked, and Erwin Servai, who was in the Gestapo. It may be that Steffahn made himself more agreeable to the older women: Fernande, who was then aged twenty-three, always remembered him as 'obnoxious'. Sister McGauley commented that he was 'not very nice to us', but she heard at the end of the war that he had been a British spy. The sentries at the camp were either very young soldiers, or war wounded or elderly reservists. Opinions on Landhauser's character and role are divided. He was born at Innsbruck and before the war had been a teacher of physical education and music. The internees who were actively involved with the local resistance knew that he was greatly feared by the Vittel underground, and had a reputation for swift reprisals. Others saw him as a genial presence, moderating the rules imposed by the regime and supporting the frequent concerts with good-natured enthusiasm. Many, however, considered that it was the Red Cross and, in particular, Mme Bouloumié who were responsible for the good conditions in the camp.

The story told by Aunt Fan about 'Mrs G.' and the disappearing tablecloths is a case in point. When those tablecloths vanished from her cupboard overnight, the hard-working and apparently hitherto blameless

Mrs G. was immediately held responsible and taken to the camp lock-up, a small well-guarded building near the gates which was often used for trouble makers. (Sofka Skipwith and five of her friends were once held there overnight, while they were investigated for being Communists). The reason Aunt Fan gives in her diary for the swift disappearance of the cloths is that underwear was still in such short supply. By chance, there survives in the archives of the Vittel Red Cross a delivery note dated 10 October 1941 from a textiles firm, for 2,000 ladies vests, 240 pairs of ladies underpants and 40 metres of percale cotton. The total bill is 53,500 francs. Attached to this note is a letter from the same company, addressed to Mme Bouloumié four days later, asking her if she would be kind enough to return the packaging material, because there is such a shortage of it and they will need it for her next order! Here at least we have evidence of Mme Bouloumié, on behalf of the Red Cross, acting to put right a shortfall in the provisions made for the prisoners, while the Kommandant responded by arresting the lady who was trying to wash the table cloths.

It was certainly the case that the Vittel camp was used for propaganda purposes. Landhauser was often seen showing visitors round, posing for photographs with groups of contented and well-fed looking internees. These photographs found their way into newspapers all over the world, especially where there were right-wing governments. Among the many visitors, the prisoners were able to recognise Ribbentrop, Abentz, the German envoy in Paris, and Scapini, the French deputy.

As with all internment camps, the Germans relied heavily on cooperative inmates to keep it running smoothly. There was an English head of the camp, assisted by a committee that organised the rotas, discipline and so on, and each area or hotel had a head, whose responsibility it was to make regular inspections to check that everyone was present. The other internees quickly learnt to recognise these women's footsteps, and to be cautious when they were nearby. There were also two enthusiastic fascists among the prisoners, who could always be relied upon to pass information to the camp authorities; the other inmates soon grew wary of them too.

Relatively few people attempted to escape from Vittel, but two friends of Sofka and Madeleine did, and they successfully reached England. The plan was simple. By the autumn of 1941, contact had been made with the Vittel resistance, so help was available from outside. Frida Stewart and Rosemary (Pat) Say, the escapees, hid in the Casino theatre after rehearsals for a show, and then wriggled out through a window. A third woman closed the window behind them from the inside, and returned inconspicuously to her hotel the next morning when the Casino was unlocked. Their absence was eventually reported, but by that time they were far away, and they were never caught.

Marcelle at Vittel.

Marcelle, a young woman from Mauritius, also escaped, but her friend Fernande never discovered what became of her.

Many more of the inmates were released because they had reached a certain age. It seems odd that the Germans felt that an English lady of fifty-nine must be kept behind barbed wire and guarded night and day by sentries, while a lady of sixty could be released and allowed to make her own way home right across France to the militarily sensitive Atlantic coast, without any sort of escort. But those were the rules, and the Biarritz area was specifically listed as a place to which internees could return. So it was that Aunt Fan was told she was free to leave Vittel in December 1941.

8

Home!

The brief, typically understated description in the diary of how Aunt Fan made her way home across occupied France is considerably amplified in her notebooks. These also contain some insights into how the all-female household managed to survive for the rest of the war:

In December 1941 I was due to be released as I would be 60 years old on the 6th. I packed my small suitcase, my sketches well hidden at the bottom with a piece of newspaper pasted over them. They would have been taken if found. Food also was not to be taken, so I took 2 packets of tea from Red Cross parcels, but under my skirt. No clothes as I left all I could to those who wanted them. I had to leave my very big French soldier's overcoat, so I only had my raincoat.

At 7 o'c on December 5th I went down to the gate, several friends with me, others were waiting at the gates. A German came and looked through my suitcase & let it pass. It was a cold morning and beginning to snow. A big Frenchman was there to take me to the station. Since the French had surrendered, the Germans could make use of the French.

I had been given a paper, written in German, saying I could travel free by train or bus, also to be given help if needed. I kept this carefully in my pocket – I had no handbag. I had also 200 francs. I could have been sent to England via Sweden, but I wanted to go home to Ciboure, St Jean de Luz.

At the station I found I could go by Dijon, changing there for a train to Bordeaux & get to Bordeaux about 11 o'c.

I got to Dijon about 11o'c and found that the Bordeaux train had left & there was no other till midday next day. I went out next morning to take a look at the town. Germans everywhere looking very happy, they all seemed to be officers with their wives and relations. I noticed some women in long fur coats. The shops were full.

The train arrived very full of people. I got a seat in a compartment full of young men, very gay and happy, returning from a football match. I think they were feeling so thankful that there was no more war for them. They looked at me suspiciously, but after I told them I was English they were quite friendly – they had won the war! In the evening the train stopped a few miles from Tours. The main line trains for Bordeaux did not always go up to Tours – there was no service to Tours and a porter came and told me I must get one going to Bordeaux. I was very glad to see a porter – it was a very small station.

He told me to take hold of his coat & we would walk in to the waiting room – no lights of course. The footballers said they would put my suitcase out of the window, but by the time I got to the window the porter [was there] & said that he would take it, & next day I would find the suitcase there. The waiting room was quite dark except for candle light on the floor. There was a bench against the wall all round and people sitting there – I found a seat on it and spent the night there. I now learnt that the line to Bordeaux had been destroyed by bombs. In the morning I went in to Tours and back – the footballers came back too, having spent the night there!

Most of the passengers had gone to Tours and did not know that those who stayed could walk a mile along the line, and would find a train waiting to go to Bordeaux. It was no good my going to Tours, so I decided to walk. I asked a Footballer if he would carry my suitcase! and said I would give him four cigarettes. He accepted at once & others offered also! They soon found the suitcase rather heavy.

We got to Bordeaux after many stops. I bribed a porter in the evening with more cigarettes to get me something from the restaurant. I had nothing to eat since the day before. The porter told me there were bedrooms also over the station, where one could stay the night. There was no train for Bayonne & St Jean de Luz till next day.

After a good night I took an early train. Having paid for the room I had no more money. In St Jean de Luz no taxis of course so I left my suitcase at a café near by and walked home to the other side of the harbour. I took a short cut up to our road, the old road between Paris and Madrid. I found the road in front of our garden door blocked by chevaux de tier [barbed wire entanglements] and a German guard patrolling. He said nothing to me. The Germans expected the English would make an attack from Spain.

We had a joyful evening at home. The suitcase was sent up and we had a very good supper, my sister, our two friends Swiss and English and our faithful maid. The Red Cross tin of stew, some beans from the garden, cups of tea and of course it was owing to my Swiss friend who we left in charge, that the house was not pillaged by the French or occupied by the Germans.

I was overjoyed to get home, to feel free and be again with my 2 sisters, 2 friends and our faithful maid. Germans patrolled in the road which was barricaded with chevaux de frise, and also they had a lookout arrangement in the garden. From this they could see a bit of the Route Nationale.

I found the family very short of food but though we all got very thin we kept well. We both lost a great deal of weight – we were reduced to 7 stone 3 or 4 I believe. But our 2 friends both died, one in February & the other 6 months later. Both quite suddenly, from heart trouble.

We had no milk butter tea or coffee, & did not get our rations or rarely. Spanish friends helped us but our diet was sardines and carrots. The sardines were split & roasted as we had no oil or fat. I used to go into the country by paths, to farms where I could get a bottle of milk or even a bit of butter, by giving an apron or a towel in exchange. Smuggling from Spain was not so easy now. We had to report at the German headquarters every week & were forbidden to go by train or bus, not to go out after dark, etc.

Then suddenly one day two French policemen came & said we were to go, within 6 days, into the unoccupied part of France, all 3 of us. We were really dismayed. We had almost no money. The American consul had left. We knew no one in the unoccupied, and how were we to transport Molly! – still quite a child mentally, and now unable to do stairs or walk much and would certainly not manage the acrobatics needed to enter a French train. The French Red Cross offered a 'lorry' to take us to the nearest spot on the boundary, 50 miles away, and I suppose would leave us beside the road.

We felt desperate. The French police gave no help. "They had their orders from the Germans." A French friend advised me to go to Biarritz & see the commandant at the hotel which was their headquarters. I had been forbidden to go anywhere by bus or train, but I took the risk & went by train and got there without trouble. At the hotel I waited in a passage, with others, opening out of the big entrance hall. Many officers were shouting orders. They looked a rough lot. One or two of us were called, sent up stairs. After 2 hours we were told to go away, as the commandant had left. I went home feeling very depressed. The same friend said to me "go again, don't give up." So I went and waited as before watching all the rough looking crowd (not the best of the German army). Then an officer crossed the hall, a very different looking man, very smart, quiet, nice manner. I thought if only I could see that man! At last I was told to go upstairs & to a certain room. In the room this man was sitting alone, another chair beside him. He spoke perfect English.

I showed him the doctor's certificates about Molly & he asked a few questions. "Had we been interned at Besançon" etc. Then he said Mademoiselle, you can stay in your house with your sisters. I felt like embracing him but luckily kept my head & only thanked him. I felt like walking on air.

It was pouring with rain. I went to the best tea shop in Biarritz & asked for a cup of tea. They were sorry, no tea or coffee, no anything, but a hot cup of "coffee" made from acorns and a small piece of very dry bread. But nothing mattered now.

Then I went to the station at St Jean & I was stopped from leaving the station & asked for my papers. Not in order they said. Something was missing. I had to stand outside the station with a German guard. There were many lookers on, as always ready to see any arrests. A young German officer came & talked to me in English, about painting. He knew I painted. He was very pleasant. Meanwhile a woman with her bike (I did not know her) had gone off to Ciboure to tell my sister what had happened, & could she produce the necessary paper. Fortunately Kathleen could produce an old paper saying we were to stay in our house. She managed to keep her thumb over the date on it, so they never found out the paper was out of date. But it worked and they let me go. All was well. We stayed. I did not know the woman – she was French – and did not try to find her for fear of getting her into trouble by helping the enemy!

Having got permission to stay in Ciboure, we were left in peace. All our English friends had gone. We had very little food, could not get our rations. I made many trips into Spain, whenever possible [as in the First World War], by quiet paths which led to "ventas". These were generally a farm, either just on the border or a little way into Spain. These were some of them well stocked with all sorts of things, food mostly, often up in the hay loft or in a barn. Some were quite small – only a shed.

One very cold day I started off to a small one on the east side of La Rhune. 3 miles on my bicycle & then 1 ½ miles walk. I had borrowed my sister's water proof boots though she didn't know it. There was a stream to cross, generally quite easy as it was full of big stones, one big one in the middle. But this day there was much more water and even a little ice about. I made a jump for the big stone but it was slippery & my feet went one way & my head the other, both in the water while I lay on the stone.

I could only get up by standing in the water. The boots already full of water, wet up to my knees. I scrambled out, sat on a bank in the sun &

emptied the boots which were lined with sheepskin, wrung out the socks & stockings & put back on the boots.

There was another stream but it had a single plank bridge & I saw sitting beside it 2 Spanish soldiers. The venta was only 20 yards from the bridge & up a hill. I generally took 2 cigarettes on these walks, saved from a Red Cross parcel. I had one in my hand and went to speak to them. They saw the cigarette at once. I asked if I could go up to the venta. I would have to be quick they said as the Capitain was expected any minute. I gave each a cigarette and they were all smiles – but did not light up on duty! I got ½ a loaf of bread, a tin of tomatoes, some oranges, but nothing else.

'Osprey.'

9

What Was Vittel?

When the Vittel camp was finally liberated by the allies in September 1944, it was suggested in some quarters that it had been a 'model camp', deliberately organised and advertised as propaganda to cover the atrocities in the concentration camps. Whether this had been the intention from the beginning, or whether the initial concern had merely been to demonstrate that the British women were now being held in good conditions, is a moot point. But certainly the types of people held at Vittel changed as the war progressed, and their destinations when they left the camp became more sinister.

At the time of Aunt Fan's release in December 1941, the camp was still largely for women with British papers, although there were also a significant number of children and some elderly men held there. Even then, Aunt Fan referred to the Grand Hotel as a 'whited sepulchre' – beautiful on the outside but rotten within.

Soon, other groups of prisoners arrived at Vittel. There was a new policy of reuniting families; men were brought from their all-male camps to join their wives and children. A small group of Soviet women appeared, and as they were not eligible for Red Cross parcels because Russia had not signed the Geneva Convention, some of the longer-established internees set up a regular collection of food for them to supplement their rations. From October 1942, Americans and dual-nationality Anglo-Americans began to arrive, and they were accommodated in the Central Hotel, on the opposite side of the perimeter road, with their own access route to the park.

In 1943, there was a fundamental change. Internees were now arriving from all over Europe, but many of them were from Poland, and an increasing number were Jews. One group of traumatised people came from Warsaw, and they were held in hotels over the road, near the Americans. Although they were allowed access to the park during the day by means of a specially built and guarded footbridge, they returned to their own quarters at night. These people already knew what was happening in the extermination camps and gradually, as they came to trust some of the British internees, their terrible experiences of the Ghetto and their fears for the future began to be told. In December 1943, in yet another new development, the Vittel camp authorities started investigating which of the internees with British papers were of Jewish descent.

Vittel now served two quite distinct purposes: it was a civilian camp for British and a few American internees, most of whom were painfully aware of the Germans' unhealthy interest in the Jews, and it was a holding bay for people being processed before being sent east. Those of the original internees who saw this most clearly tried desperately to make the outside world take action, but to no avail. For her efforts to save these people, Sofka Skipwith was eventually honoured with the title 'Righteous Among The Gentiles'.

Only a very few of the Jews held at Vittel survived. A baby was smuggled out through the wire one night and cared for in the town. A young man was hidden in a room in the Grand Hotel (coincidentally, the one next to that in which Aunt Fan had previously lived) and only emerged when the camp was liberated. One prisoner married a Christian internee, but the camp authorities refused to accept it, so marriages of convenience offered no hope.

The first transports of prisoners from Vittel seem to have been of a group of women and children from North Africa, who were taken to Bergen-Belsen. A group of survivors of the Warsaw Ghetto who had hoped to be allowed to travel to South America were told that their papers were not in order and they were arrested and interrogated. On 17 April 1944, local workmen brought word into the camp that a train with sealed windows was waiting at the railway station. Over the next 24 hours, several of the Polish Jews attempted to commit suicide, but few succeeded; however critically injured, most of these desperate people were forced to wait for their fate with the others. One internee remembered for years afterwards the sickening thud when a woman flung herself down a stairwell; other people jumped from upstairs windows. April 18th marked the first of several deportations from Vittel to Auschwitz.

These events had a traumatic effect on those trying to help. Sister McGauley's recollections stand for many:

Towards the end of June 1944 we heard that the bridge between the camp and the school villa had been closed ... Mothers came to the Little Sisters and begged them to adopt their children even though it meant never seeing them again. That night many children had their wrists slashed, took poison etc, in an attempt to end their lives. It was heart breaking and it was at this point that I felt I couldn't take any more.

The Continental [Hotel] was quite near the road and from the windows on the top floor we saw most of those families going off in the cattle trucks to their deaths – the children who were too ill to travel followed afterwards.

The final days of the Vittel camp were chaotic. In the face of the Allied advance and the increased activity of the local resistance movements, the Germans and their collaborators fled. Most were shot in cold blood in the surrounding fields. For ten days the camp was without officers or administration, until the town and its prisoners were liberated on 12 September by General Leclerc and the American army.

Postscript

Everyone who survived being held in a camp during the war was scarred by the experience, each in their own way.

Most of the Besançon and Vittel internees were repatriated initially to England, either in a prisoner exchange in the summer of 1944, which involved a dangerous week-long train journey to the Spanish border and then on to Lisbon where they boarded a ship for Liverpool, or after liberation via a transit camp in France.

Sofka Skipwith's husband was killed in action, and it was only her close friendships with fellow-internees and the care she received at the Vittel camp hospital which helped her to come to terms with her loss. The things she witnessed while she was interned led to her becoming a convinced Communist.

Madeleine White (Steinberg) dedicated herself to publicising the story of the Jews held at Vittel.

Sister McGauley returned to her Congregation, and ended her working life in England.

Samuel Hales never properly recovered from his internment, although he lived to be eighty-five.

The Red Cross intervened on Fernande's behalf, and she was freed early in 1942 because her father was Italian. But she spent the next two years in occupied France, and the Germans tried hard to persuade her to relinquish her British citizenship.

For Aunt Fan, her year at Besançon and Vittel was part of the wider picture of the German occupation. After her release, there were still another three years of near-starvation, and the deaths of her two close friends, before France was liberated. At the end of the war, Kathleen and Fan were repatriated to England, but were so malnourished that they were given double rations while they recovered. They then returned home to Ciboure. Molly died aged sixty, Kathleen in her eighties, and Aunt Fan finally agreed, regretfully, to move to England when she was in her mid nineties. I met her when she was 101. A truly remarkable lady.

of us talking broken German to him.
It was very difficult to get all the
necessary conditions at the same
moment. Two out of my three
letters reached their port.

waiting to start
for Vittel.

A self-portrait in Aunt Fan's diary.

Bibliography

Primary Sources

Miss M. Bayliss: memoir written after her return to the UK. (Imperial War Museum, 96/49/1)

Mr James Fox: collected materials from his private archives. (Personal Communication)

Mlle Sonia Gumuchian: recollections and family archives relating to the camps. (Personal Communication)

E. Hales: unpublished diary of her internment, courtesy of her grandsons John and Christopher Hales. (Personal Communication)

S. Hales: 'Besançon', article for *Otago Boys High School Magazine*, April 1946. (Archives of Le Centre de Documentation, Musée de la Résistance et de la Déportation, Besançon. 325.7 FC 25 HAL)

ICRC: 'The Report of the International Red Cross Delegation to Besançon, 28th January 1941'. (Geneva, February 1941)

Sister P. McGauley: memoir written in 1999. (Imperial War Museum, 99/82/1)

Miscellaneous Papers. (Le Centre de Documentation, Musée de la Résistance et de la Déportation, Besançon)

Mrs Rita Muller: memoirs and material mostly written in 2003 & 2005. (Imperial War Museum, 05/71/1)

Mme Fernande Oldfield: unpublished French memoir of her internment. (Personal Communication)

Mrs Sofka Skipwith: memoirs written after internment. (Imperial War Museum, 92/31/1)

Mme Madeleine Steinberg: correspondence relating to the nomination of Sofka Skipwith as 'Righteous Among The Gentiles'. (Imperial War Museum, 93/31/1)

Frida Stewart and Rosemary Say: article for *The New Statesman and Nation*, March 28th, 1942. (Imperial War Museum, 05/71/1)

Mrs Annie Strong: *Stalag 142 dans La Caserne Vauban*. (Typescript in the archives of Le Centre de Documentation, Musée de la Résistance et de la Déportation, Besançon (2005))

W. G. Webb: memories of the arrest of his mother and sister, and release of his mother, and summary of his mother's account of her internment at Besançon. (Imperial War Museum, 04/13/1)

Secondary Sources

Azéma, J-P. *From Munich to the Liberation: 1938-1944. The Cambridge History of Modern France.* (Cambridge: Cambridge University Press and Maison des Sciences de l'Homme, 1984). Originally published in French as *De Munich à la Libération, 1938-1944.* (Paris: Editions du Seuil, 1979)

Brönnimann, S. *The Global Climate Anomaly 1940-1942.* Weather 60 (2005), 336-342.

Dutriez, R. *Quand La Caserne Vauban, à Besançon, était le plus grand couvent du monde ... décembre 1940 – mai 1941.* Journal des Victimes de la Guerre et des Anciens Combattants du Doubs 325 (1991), pp. 1 & 6.

Horton, R. *Les Civils Britanniques internes en Europe entre 1939 et 1945.* (Belgium: Sabel Print, 1995)

Miscellaneous Papers supplied by the Hôpital St Jacques, Besançon.

Miscellaneous Papers supplied by the Maison du Patrimoine, Vittel.

Moore, Bob, and Fedorowich, Kent (eds). *Prisoners of War and their Captors in World War II.* (Oxford: Berg, 1996)

Poinsot, C. *Le Camp des Internes de Vittel, 1941-1944.* (Vittel: Maison du Patrimoine, 2004)

Skipwith, S. *Sofka: The Autobiography of a Princess.* (London: Hart-Davis, 1968)

Steinberg, M. *Témoinage: Paris, Besançon, Vittel 1941-1944, une Internée Civile Britannique Témoin Indirect de la Fin du Ghetto de Varsovie.* Revue d'Histoire de la Shoah 180 (2004), 315-350.

Vichard, P. (ed.). *Le Patrimoine Hospitalier du Doubs. A l'Initiative de l'Union Hospitalière du Sud-Est et de la Federation Hospitalière de France.* (Besançon: Neo-Typo, 2005)

Zinovieff, S. *Red Princess: A Revolutionary Life.* (London: Granta Publications, 2007)

ALSO AVAILABLE FROM
AMBERLEY PUBLISHING

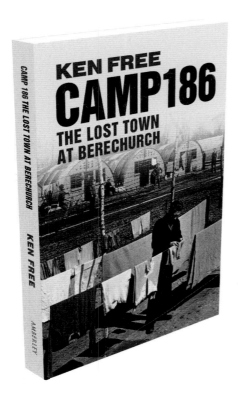

CAMP 186
THE LOST TOWN
AT BERECHURCH

Ken Free

Price: £16.99
ISBN: 978-1-4456-0012-3
Binding: PB
Extent: 160 pages

Available from all good bookshops or order direct
from our website www.amberleybooks.com

ALSO AVAILABLE FROM
AMBERLEY PUBLISHING

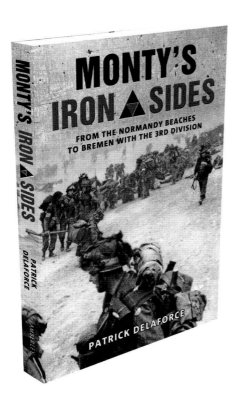

MONTY'S IRON SIDES
FROM THE NORMANDY
BEACHES TO BREMEN WITH
THE 3RD DIVISION

Patrick Delaforce

Price: £14.99
ISBN: 978-1-84868-819-3
Binding: PB
Extent: 224 pages

Available from all good bookshops or order direct
from our website www.amberleybooks.com

ALSO AVAILABLE FROM
AMBERLEY PUBLISHING

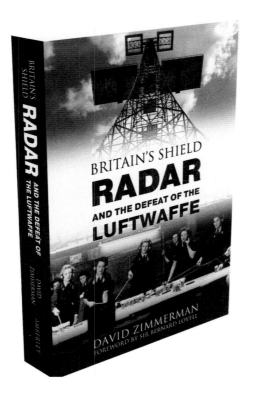

BRITAIN'S SHIELD
RADAR AND THE DEFEAT
OF THE LUFTWAFFE

David Zimmerman

Price: £18.99
ISBN: 978-1-4456-0061-1
Binding: PB
Extent: 352c pages

Available from all good bookshops or order direct
from our website www.amberleybooks.com